I was awake, my arms and neck clammy, a cold sweat drenched every pore of my body. I knew this was an omen—a warning that life as I had known it before was about to change . . .

I floated a dozen feet in the air to question the Guide. I had to remind myself: Remember Shawn, this is happening sometime in the future—I looked around for a calendar. There was one on the opposite wall. It said **April 2044**.

I closed my eyes and tried to shake away the aberrations of my travel with the Guide. I was in a classroom. There were twenty-five kids. I scanned the children. No one was moving around. There were no taps, no hums, no one weaving in their seats. I looked at them again. They looked normal enough. In fact, too normal. They were all robust and healthy, all about the same height and weight, all had similar hair colors . . . and eyes the same shade of greenish blue. Row after row of girls with Heather Locklear noses and boys with cheekbones of Don Johnson. They all basically looked the same: PERFECT CHILDREN!

MORE PROPHECIES
FOR THE COMING
MILLENNIUM

SHAWN ROBBINS
and Edward Susman

AVON BOOKS ◆ NEW YORK

VISIT OUR WEBSITE AT
http://AvonBooks.com

MORE PROPHECIES FOR THE COMING MILLENNIUM is an original
publication of Avon Books. This work has never before appeared in book
form.

AVON BOOKS
A division of
The Hearst Corporation
1350 Avenue of the Americas
New York, New York 10019

First Avon Books Printing: December 1996

AVON TRADEMARK REG. U.S. PAT. OFF. AND IN OTHER COUNTRIES, MARCA
REGISTRADA, HECHO EN U.S.A.

Printed in the U.S.A.

RA   10   9   8   7   6   5   4   3   2   1

CONTENTS

MORE PROPHECIES
FOR THE COMING
MILLENNIUM

1

A HEROINE'S REWARD OR FIFTY YEARS IN THE MINES OF JUPITER

NABYLA GUERRERO COHANE, GREAT-GRANDDAUGHTER OF a Baseball Hall of Fame slugger, granddaughter of a U.S. senator from Cuba, daughter of a Jewish-Arab oil merchant from Palestine—now an AWOL contract asteroid mapper—peered down the sight of her self-manufactured rifle and waited.

If all the ifs worked out, in just a few brief moments she would become the architect of the greatest event in human history, overshadowing everything her illustrious ancestors had done before her.

Nabyla studied the hologram out of the corner of her eye, the heat of the two suns coaxing a bead of perspiration from her forehead. She was aware of the moisture as it followed a highway down the strands of her dark hair, then left the raven road to drip onto her cheek before it rolled down to her neck.

She willed her mouth to form saliva and swallowed

1

to moisten her throat. *How many bizarre microbes on this world are already fighting my immune system?* she wondered. Her fears of contracting some hopelessly deadly germ were mollified by the knowledge that over the past twenty years and numerous illegal excursions to the planet surface, there had been no reported casualties due to whatever was different about the air she breathed.

Of course, there was the mission that left behind the corpses of crewmen who had failed to protect themselves against the marauding fauna that roamed the ground and flew in the air on this planet. Information had even been broadcast through space over the past two decades, from freebooters like herself, to give Nabyla enough data to know that the less movement you made, the better were your chances of survival. The birdlike creatures were the worst. They could spot movement a time zone away, it seemed, and swoop in at impossible speeds to spear you with their elongated swordlike beaks or tear you to shreds with fifteen-inch-long talons.

She nervously checked the hologram display just to the left front of her field of vision. The display was no sophisticated video game, but Nabyla's buffer between success, triumph, and fame, and becoming dinner for one of half a dozen creatures that prowled menacingly on the plains below or hovered dangerously in the skies above her.

From the point of view of the enormous creatures above, the only thing abnormal on the ground was a tiny wire protruding between rocks on a cliff ledge. The wire was Nabyla's eyes and ears; the advanced fiber-optic antenna and transponder translated movement on the plain and in the air to a computer, which created the holograms. Nabyla wondered if her pilot orbiting the planet had her position fixed and was ready to make the grab if she succeeded in locating one of the humanoids.

Twenty years of explorations by freebooters had failed to bring back to earth a live specimen of the Centauris. No one dared to report a failure or to bring back a dead alien. Earth governments discouraged the idea of bringing back specimens because many felt it was akin to kidnapping or slavery. Attempts to finance missions succumbed to philosophical disunity. The only positive—depending on one's viewpoint—thing done was to develop intergalactic laws which said that killing an intelligent humanoid anywhere in the universe was punishable by prevailing laws of the nation having jurisdiction over the offense. In some cases that could mean death, but in others it merely meant a fifty-year term working in the Jupiter moon mines.

Nabyla shuddered to think what would happen to her and the crew if she returned empty-handed. She calculated that she'd been missing for 25 years, and if she failed to come back with a living, breathing Centauri as an exhibit, the government-industry agencies that had sent her into space in the first place would throw her into some prison for eternity—and that was only after the corporations that had sponsored her and her team had drained every last space-dollar from her body.

This could have been the dumbest thing I've ever done, Nabyla thought to herself, hoping the occasional static in her ear wasn't concealing critical information. She also wondered what kinds of tiny creatures that crawled on the surface, the planet's equivalent of ants, mosquitoes, parasites, and worms, were attaching themselves to her boots, reflective pants, and shirts. There were times when she thought she felt something crawling on her skin, but suppressed the desire to scratch for fear that even a little motion would bring one of those soaring creatures upon her. As she lay in the blind, she put her faith in the ship's medications, hoping they could handle the weird diseases she was confident she was contracting.

Maybe capturing a Centauri alive was the same as kidnapping, but Nabyla figured it was worth it. Even staid scientific organizations were offering huge rewards if a Centauri could be "persuaded" to travel to Earth. Of course, no one had even gotten close enough to a Centauri to discuss travel to another planet. There was no knowledge of language; no knowledge of customs; no knowledge of the strange humanoid race at all.

Despite being hundreds of thousands of years ahead of the Centauris in technology, there were incredible problems in capturing members of the alien race: If you got within hollering distance, they took off and vanished; if you stunned them from a distance, the wily, enormous, and deadly monsters aroam would snatch the body and turn it into a meal before you could get to it or other aliens would carry their zonked comrade into their lair; but most annoying was the fact that the aliens always seemed to know when they were being hunted and where the attackers were—which sometimes proved fatal to the freebooter.

Even so, Nabyla and her crew figured that capturing an alien was a whole lot more fun than spending their forty-year contract watching the asteroids between Mars and Jupiter to see if any got knocked off course and were heading toward Earth. For seventy years, patrols had zipped back and forth across the Asteroid Belt looking for likely candidates which could destroy the Earth, tracking them, then leading the rocket engine teams to the unruly rock. Three years into their contract, Nabyla and her team had enough of the dullness of asteroid-mapping and headed off to the Centauri system, seeking more exhilarating game.

Now Nabyla was ready; all she had to do was wait for that history-making shot with her rapid-fire stun gun. Her idea: stun all the humanoids in the party, then waste a couple of the monsters with her laser. If all went well, she'd pinpoint the location of the aliens so her ship could swoop in, pick them up, and be on their way back to Earth with a prize that would make them rich and famous.

She looked into the treelike area at the edge of the plains, perhaps two thousand yards away—in easy range of her rifle, which was accurate up to ten thousand yards. She sighted on the space between two trees. "That almost looks like a path," she said. But as she gazed down the firing line, the edges of the forest and of her field of vision became hazy; the scene darkened. Confused and alarmed, Nabyla checked the hologram, now blinking on and off. Her vision abruptly went dark, and just as suddenly a bright flash of light surrounded her.

I sat up in bed, aware that my field of vision was narrowing, as if I were looking down a long pipe that stretched to infinity. The scene which had been close enough to touch was moving away, faster and faster. The contact with the thoughts of the young woman on that strange planet became fuzzy, then incoherent, then drifted into nothingness. The tube grew darker and longer; the light at the end of the pipe grew smaller and smaller, and was tinged with an ominous reddish brown hue—the color of dried blood. There was now only a pinpoint of light at the distant end of the pipe. That light, too, blinked out.

I was awake, my arms and neck clammy, a cold sweat drenching every pore of my body. I knew this was an omen—a warning that life as I had known it before was about to change.

If this was just a dream, I knew a nightmare was beginning.

2

THE RETURN OF THE PSYCHIC'S GUIDE

I SWALLOWED HARD AND SQUEEZED THE RECEIVER AS IF it were a life preserver. Intellectually, I realized that I was going through another of the panic attacks I knew all too well. I told myself, "Relax, Shawn, relax. In fifteen seconds the phone will ring. In twenty seconds you'll talk to him, and within thirty seconds all this will be over."

But somewhere between the R2-D2 noises and that first ring all I heard was the static over the line. A faint noise that connected me to another world, another dimension, another time that was far away and very, very far below me. The world seemed to open beneath my feet and fall away, as if some giant pothole had opened up on the Greenwich Village street and had swallowed my world, and now was about to devour me.

I was suspended over the abyss that dropped away to darkness. I could feel my head begin to spin and vertigo envelop me.

My heart beat faster and faster. It pounded so hard I thought I would have to hold on to my chest to keep the organ inside my body. I could feel my lips go dry, and that space above my chin get damp with perspiration.

Oh God, oh God, please answer the phone, I prayed to myself. I suddenly had the harrowing thought—*what if he's on the phone? What will I do then?* Finally—wasn't it an hour—the brrrrrr on the ring a thousand miles away echoed in the phone. But the responding click of an answer wasn't there. Another ring. Still no response.

I stuck a finger in my mouth and began chewing the nail. "He's got to be home. He's got to be there." I willed him to be home. "If I've got any psychic power at all," I told myself, "he will pick up the phone."

The machine clicked and a hum replaced the ring. My heart sank. The answering machine! Oh no, not the answering machine. The sweet young voice began its cheery hello. "I haven't got time for this," I snarled at the machine. Defiantly I pushed the button for his voice mail— how I loathe voice mail. "That's what I'll tell him. I'll tell him how much I hate voice mail. What an affront voice mail is to . . ."

"Hello."

"Me, to mankind, to . . ."

"Er. Shawn?"

"Oh God, oh God, thank God it's you. . . ." My head stopped spinning; the vacant space beneath my feet became the floor of my apartment. I could, however, still feel and hear the throbbing in my chest. I was glad there was no one around to take my blood pressure.

"Shawn, calm down. It's okay. What's going on?"

"Oh, Ed. He's back. He's back. At least I think it's him. What am I going to do? And how did you know it was me?"

"Well, that's simple. It's after nine o'clock. Nobody calls me after nine o'clock. In fact, the only one who gets calls here after nine is my daughter. So if someone wanted to call me, then it had to be you. Simple."

I sat down and picked up a cigarette. "Well, I think you knew it was me because you are psychic, too. I've told you that before, and it's true. You are psychic; you just don't want to admit it."

"Shawn, we've discussed this too many times for me to argue with you. I know that you are psychic, and if you think I'm psychic, well, I'll just accept it. So, what's the crisis?"

"The Guide. I saw him again."

There was a silence at the other end. It took a long time before I could admit that the Guide existed, and even today I'm not sure he does. He appears to my subconscious, but his words and his looks and his demeanor have to be drawn from me, and my friend and cowriter Ed Susman is one person who can perform that magic. That's his psychic gift. He has it, but like so many others with the gift, he won't truly accept it. He calls his good luck coincidences or just routine journalism, but he always seems to know when to make that extra phone call or whom to talk to in a crowded bus station or which door to knock on one more time to make the story work. Take it from someone who knows psychic phenomena, he has it.

Ed's voice had changed. I detected a scratch in it. "He's back, huh? How do you know that you saw him? Are you sure you weren't just dreaming?"

"It's nine forty-five, Ed. You know I'm wide-awake at this hour. It's like the middle of the day to me. I haven't even gone out yet to have dinner. I saw him."

"Shawn, I thought you said he was gone. You haven't had contact with him in over a year. He was out of here. Now you are saying he's back?"

"It wasn't a dream, Ed. He was here—and he was wearing a business suit!"

For more than fifteen years, Ed and I have worked together, doing stories mainly for the tabloid press. One of the reasons we've managed to get along so well is because he has a psychic sense. Even if he doesn't use it or admit his own psychic abilities, he's open-minded about the powers of others.

He tells me that he's seen psychics at work, and their abilities make the hair on the back of his neck stand straight out. And I gained his lasting respect—he'd told me so a number of times—when he was injured playing basketball.

I was talking to him on the phone, and something about

our conversation didn't seem right. Ed was his congenial self, but I don't know if it was something in his voice that tipped me off or just my psychic tuning picking something up.

"Are you all right?" I asked in the middle of the conversation.

"Sure."

"I just got the feeling that something was wrong. That maybe you had hurt yourself."

There was dead air. "Oh," he said, a catch in his voice, "I hurt my leg playing basketball last night."

"Your left knee?"

A long pause. "Yup," very softly.

"Umm, you know, Ed, I really think you are going to need surgery. You should see a doctor."

His voice brightened. "Actually, Shawn, I saw a doctor this morning. He thinks that with a bit of exercise and rehabilitation the knee will be just fine."

"Oh," I said, "that's great." I felt good for Ed, but something told me that the doctor was wrong.

A month later he had a massive chunk of medial meniscus cartilage arthroscopically removed from that left knee. Ask him about that incident; he'll tell you it's true.

Thanks to his reporting skills and his knowledge of psychic powers, Ed has understood how to get the best stories from the numerous psychics about whom he writes. I've talked to a number of them myself, and we all marvel at the way he can get us to reach into our subconscious and recall what we need to make predictions or, in my case, recover visions. That's why I went to him for help in writing the first book, and now in writing this one as well.

Now I needed his help again. As desperate as I was to reveal the visions I saw at the shrine of Kateri Tekakwitha in upstate New York, the new scenes that terrified my subconscious and near conscious were even more compelling.

"What do you mean, Shawn," Ed said. "That he was wearing a business suit? I thought he told us he was most comfortable in the summer regalia of an Iroquois warrior."

"I don't know," I told him. "It freaked me out so much

that as soon as I saw him in the Armani duds I lost contact.''

''You saw him long enough to know he was wearing Armani?'' Ed said, with more than a hint of incredulity in his voice.

''A girl in New York knows these things,'' I assured him.

He laughed heartily. I even managed a chuckle despite the fact that I was scared to death.

Ed stopped laughing and his entire demeanor changed. ''Shawn, why do you think he came back to you? Are you sure that he really left? Or was he trying to tell you something important that you were trying to block from your mind? Think about it very carefully, very carefully.''

I'm the easiest person in the world to put into a light trance, light enough to remain conscious enough to hold on to the telephone receiver and yet deep enough to allow my psychic thoughts to separate from my consciousness. I began to tremble; tears welled in my eyes. ''It's terrible, just terrible. The world is going to end, the world is going to end, the world is going to end . . .''

3

THE USE OF GENES CREATES A PERFECT CHILD TO ABANDON

I DUTIFULLY LISTENED TO THE TEACHER AS SHE CARE-fully outlined the algebra problem on the blackboard. Years of maturity and growth had not helped me one iota in understanding what in the world the x's meant or why the y's were significant.

I swiveled, as I floated a dozen feet in the air to question the Guide. He placed a finger to his lips, leaned toward me, and said, "The lesson is not important. Look around the classroom." He was whispering, as if the children and the teacher could hear us. I had to remind myself: *Remember Shawn, this is happening sometime in the future*—I looked around for a calendar. There was a calendar on the wall, opposite the blackboard. The calendar showed a picture of a nebula in brilliant oranges and purples. The bottom part had normal boxes and the month, April, and the year, 2044.

My first thought was: *Fifty years from now the teachers are still going to be using blackboards and chalk and eras-*

11

ers. What happened to the computer generation? I looked around the room. The children weren't taking notes. They were silently tapping information directly into keyboards that were part of their desks.

I magically lowered myself to look over the shoulder of one of the children—they must have been eleven or twelve years old—figures appeared in midair in front of the child. My mouth dropped open in awe. The Guide appeared nearby, "Heads-up display. Obviously you are not driving hot cars or F-16s." I watched transfixed and symbols popped into display, roughly copying what the teacher wrote on the board.

Slowly I floated back to my position at ceiling level and talked excitedly to the Guide. "The blackboard is still necessary," I told him, "because the teacher still has to have control of the class. They need to be looking at her and she needs to look at them. A computer-generated image wouldn't have the same effect on the class. What worked in the nineteenth-century one-room schoolhouse is still the best form of education in the twenty-first century."

The Guide nodded in agreement. "That's very profound, Shawn. It's very observant, and, of course, it has almost nothing to do with why I've brought you here. Take another look around. You're a psychic. Use that psychic ability; look into the room and see what's happening," he said, spreading his hands toward the twenty or so children intently trying to solve the next puzzle of x's and y's and integers.

I closed my eyes and tried to shake away the aberrations of my travel with the Guide and just concentrate on the room. I opened my eyes and looked around. There were five rows of children, five children in each row. Twenty-five kids. I watched as the lesson progressed, and one thing struck me at once. Every time I have ever lectured in high school or college or in an auditorium, I never have to wait long before I can spot a person with attention deficit disorder. He or she is the one fidgeting in his seat, or tapping his fingers, or bouncing his leg up and down.

Attention deficit disorder became the disability of the decade in the 1990s. There was always a debate as to whether

ADD really existed in children or was just simply children being children in crowded classrooms. Several studies seemed to correlate higher incidences of ADD with more students in the room. The skeptics said that teachers who might have been able to handle an occasionally disruptive student in a smaller group of children could not cope with two, three, or four children who were getting out of their seats, impulsively talking to classmates, drumming their fingers. Teachers demanded that something be done about these students and sent the kids to visit the vice principal. The school authorities now had to deal with handfuls of these children and called in the parents and told them something had to be done. What the teachers had in mind was to put the kids on medications, usually stimulants, which allowed the children to focus on their studies. The most prevalent drug was Ritalin, and the Ritalin generation was launched in the 1990s. Virtually every classroom had at least one child on the drug. While it apparently kept order in the classroom, there had always been doubts about whether Ritalin actually helped students get better grades.

The problem with ADD was that just about every parent who had a disruptive child in school was advised to drug the kid. In Utah, where strict Mormon families had a problem in dealing with disruptive children—usually boys— sometimes ten percent or more of the children were on Ritalin. For parents, it became a question of: Am I a failure as a parent because my son is a hell-raiser at school? or Gosh, does my little darling have a real organic disorder that can be controlled by wonderful medication? Most parents opted for Door Number Two.

I remember going to a holiday program at my nephew's school and watching as this six-year-old classmate bounced from one leg to the other as the chorus sang. Every child stood still and participated as a unit, but this one youngster stood out, weaving back and forth.

That was the first time I recognized ADD myself. I thought back to my own elementary school and recalled that there were always one or two students in the room who were never still, never knew where we were in the lesson, and were constant disciplinary problems in school, but outside of class they were the best friends a person could have. My closest friends growing up, I'm sure, had ADD—I fed off their vital energy.

Most researchers in the ADD field suggested that as many as five percent of children had ADD. That's one out of twenty—or about one or two in a classroom.

The Guide entered my thoughts. "You are getting warm, Shawn," he said. "By the way, you should know that by the year 2004, just a couple of years after the Human Genome Project was completed, most researchers were convinced that ADD was a genetically regulated syndrome."

I interrupted his incursion into my brain, "Human Genome Project?"

"Yes, the government-sponsored mapping of the entire human DNA structure, base pair by base pair—all three billion base pairs," he explained.

The numbers he spouted were fantastic, but I hadn't been living in a bubble for the past decade. I recalled some mentions of the project, especially as scientists in the 1990s seemed to be identifying one new gene after another.

The Guide went on, "Even though most scientists were convinced that ADD was genetic in nature, it took until 2018 before the work finally delivered concrete proof and identified which genes were responsible for ADD and which genes could be turned on and off with chemicals and gene therapy to correct the condition."

Again, from my perch above the classroom, I scanned the children. No one was moving around. There were no taps, no hums, no one weaving in their seats. "Wow!" I thought, doing some quick nonalgebraic mathematics. "Within twenty-six years—2018 to 2044—science had figured out how to protect kids against ADD. No," I corrected myself, "these children are twelve years old. It's possible that those breakthroughs occurred around 2032." I had solved the mystery the Guide had presented me. I was really proud of myself. But my self-assured smile faded as I turned toward him.

"Look again, Shawn. It's right there in front of you."

Perplexed, I looked at the children again. I strained to see what was so obvious. The children looked normal enough. In fact, they looked too normal. They were all robust and healthy; they were all about the same height and weight; all had similar hair colors—blondish to strawberry blond.

I let myself glide to the teacher's perspective and looked at row after row of girls with Emma Samms heart-shaped faces and Heather Locklear noses, and boys with the cheekbones of Don Johnson and the chin of Cary Grant. I looked into row after row of eyes the same shade of greenish blue. They weren't twins—far from it, because there were all kinds of skin tones, from porcelain to amber—but they all basically looked the same.

Unable to understand what kind of horrendous experiment was going on with the children, I turned on the Guide—in fury and in horror. "What the hell is going on?"

"Frankly, Shawn," he said, "I'm surprised it took twenty years for the abuses to begin. The more cynical in the field of genetic engineering expected it sooner, but the forces of good held out for longer than one would have normally predicted."

The Guide smiled, leaned back as if he were sitting in an easy chair instead of floating in air, and began another of his history lessons. The Guide let me believe that he was at least five hundred years old, so history was his forte. I often wondered how he could recall all the events over hundreds of years when I had trouble remembering who was president before Jimmy Carter.

It took human scientists until the nineteenth century before someone figured out that genetics controlled growth of animals, plants, and humans. Gregor Mendel, who is today considered the father of genetics, was the first person to figure out and publish a rough idea of how traits were inherited and passed along from generation to generation. His landmark works were presented at scientific meetings in 1865 and 1866 and were promptly forgotten, never to be discussed again for a generation.

It could be argued that science lost a generation in the field of genetics because Mendel won an election in his monastery and became an abbot. So instead of tending his garden and following nature's course of events more closely, Mendel had to figure out how best to operate the monastery.

About 1900, three groups of scientists, working independently from each other, concentrated on determining genetic traits in plants, and then, when they checked the sparse literature on the subject, found out that Mendel had beaten them by a generation. But their work confirmed Mendel's laws of genetics.

Another fifty years passed before scientists determined that DNA was responsible for hereditary, and it wasn't until the year Americans stepped on the Moon and the Mets won the World Series—1969—that anyone managed to isolate a gene. From Mendel to the isolation of a gene took more than one hundred years. It took less than one more year for researchers to begin tampering with nature. An artificial gene was created in 1970, and the first successful attempt at genetic engineering occurred in 1973.

In 1984, the Human Genome Project got its birth when academic and government scientists decided that a map of the human genome would be incredibly useful in helping people understand the functioning of the body and to develop ways in which genes could be manipulated to rid the species of unwanted side effects of evolution—such as disease. Eventually scientists from the United States, Europe, and Japan joined in the effort to map the human genome— the description of all three billion base pairs that make up all the genes that make humans human.

About one hundred thousand different genes are required to make one human being; these genes enhance the production of chemicals which eventually determine how we look, how we live, how we learn, and how we die. Actually there isn't a whole lot of difference between humans and horses or humans and pigs—more than ninety percent of the genes are the same. It's that other ten percent that make humans human, horses horses, and pigs pigs.

A lot of intensive work and a few billion dollars went into creating the map of the genome system, the object being that once we knew the map and code of each gene, then we could determine what each set of these base pairs meant to the functioning of the body and which ones were normal and which ones were not.

It was a daunting task. Long before scientists had made much headway into figuring out how to control disease, genetic ethicists were already debating and arguing about how the evil that lurks in the heart of man could use the information in the genome to divert the efforts of scientists who were working to check disease into the hands of speculators and the greedy and the wealthy who would look for ways of turning genes into fountains of youth or deliverers of beauty and perfection.

The critics harkened back to the days of the Third Reich, when Hitler and his legions tried to forge the master race by "encouraging" the mating of the Reich's children with others of pure Aryan blood in an effort to produce more and more perfect sons for the Fatherland. Genetically, it was crude work.

Only five years after the completion of the Human Genome Project, the search began in earnest for ways of making a lot of money by creating genetically engineered beings.

And, included in that search, was the fuzzy idea that geneticists might be able to create perfect people—people who would be precise copies of the best traits of humankind. It was a dream that was no longer the mad ravings of fanatics but among the possibilities of science.

That was the background for the beginning of the Cloningers or the Clone People.

Science and industry both have to accept blame for the abuse of genetic alteration science. The medical scientists, motivated by the desire to end the scourge of cancer and heart disease and diabetes and pneumonia and a thousand other illnesses, set out to find the genes that caused the diseases, or more importantly, to find the reason why some genes that kept a disease such as cancer in check no longer worked.

Billions of dollars were spent around the world tracking down aberrations of the p53 gene, a so-called traffic cop. When the cop was on the job, breast cancer and other cancers never developed in the body. But if some mutation occurred, the cop went to sleep on the job and gave cancer cells a chance to grow and to kill.

In the late 1990s, the p53 gene in women with breast cancer was completely sequenced—first by a team of Swedish researchers. They found more than fifty different mutations in the gene, and each mutation affected how the cancer grew and how it could be treated.

It took researchers thirty-five years before they had squeezed all the information about the p53 gene mutations out of the laboratory and put it into practical use. That's why it took until about 2040 before breast cancer and ovarian cancer were listed in encyclopedias along with smallpox as eradicated diseases.

The Guide nudged me psychically and again that classroom came into focus. "If you were to watch this classroom for a week, you would see that something else is missing," he said.

I viewed the children and noticed nothing significant. I turned to the Guide, trying to put on my most perplexed countenance. He helped. "What you won't see is any child taking out an inhaler filled with a bronchodilator to control an attack of asthma."

"Hmm," I thought aloud, "there were always one or two kids I knew in school who carried those inhalers with them everywhere. They were lifelines in case of an attack."

"You know why you aren't going to see inhalers in this classroom?"

I could think of several reasons: implants to prevent attacks, vaccines, long-lasting medications, improved pollution controls . . .

"Nope," said the Guide, his arms behind his head, taking the attitude of I-know-something-you-don't-know. "Asthma disappeared because Napoleon left Elba."

"Huh?"

"It's a long story," he said.

Despised by his countrymen and a renegade as far as the rest of Europe was concerned, Napoleon—defeated more by the cold winter of Russia than by better soldiering—fled to the island of Elba, off the coast of Italy. But he didn't stay in exile there very long. On March 13, 1815, Napoleon left Elba, returned to France, and within three weeks had managed to rally Frenchmen behind him.

But Napoleon still had to face the combined forces of England and Prussia, and the powerful armies met at Waterloo in Belgium. The resulting defeat left Napoleon without support even in France. Eventually the British exiled him to the lonely, bleak island of St. Helena, in the middle of the Atlantic Ocean.

But so fearful were the British that Napoleon would escape this island prison, that the British seized every conceivable island in the ocean from whence a liberation party could be launched. Napoleon had proved himself not only to be a master general, but also a master politician. Once he was back in France, the British had no doubt that they would have to battle Napoleon's armies one more time.

Among the rocks that were occupied by British garrisons was the island of Tristan da Cunha, a volcanic peak even more isolated from the rest of the world than was St. Helena. In fact, Tristan, discovered by a Portuguese explorer hundreds of years before and then promptly forgotten by the rest of the world, is fifteen hundred miles from St. Helena, and St. Helena is eight hundred miles from the nearest land point in equatorial Africa.

Why anyone thought that a Napoleonic rescue could be mounted from Tristan da Cunha shows how paranoid the British were that Napoleon's admirers would try any means to free him.

A small garrison was landed on Tristan da Cunha, and the garrison and their families eventually grew into a small community, living frugally and subsisting on local crops and imported sheep. Napoleon died in 1852, but Britain continued to maintain Tristan da Cunha as a part of a far-flung empire upon which the sun never set.

As remote as Tristan is, and as uninviting—planes can't land on the island, and it has no decent harbors—the island experiences almost no visitation from the outside world. The population grew to a size—three hundred—that was the maximum sustainable on the steep volcanic mountainsides. For the next one hundred years, Tristan did very little to make itself known to the rest of mankind.

The most notable activity came in the 1920s, when Ernest Shackleton, the renowned explorer of Antarctica, visited while en route to another adventure on the frozen continent.

In 1960, the volcano that created Tristan da Cunha erupted, and the British government evacuated the entire population. The Tristan islanders were taken to southern England, where they stayed for two years. When sociologists, anthropologists, genealogists, and virtually every other scientist realized what a treasure trove of data was represented by the arrival of this otherwise isolated group of people—really kept apart from the rest of the world for one hundred and fifty years—they descended upon the islanders with notebooks, microphones, needles, and syringes.

One of the interesting findings was that among Tristan islanders was the largest percentage of people with asthma in the known world. Fully thirty percent of the people on the island had asthma, more than double or triple the rest of the world's most affected communities.

After two years of an unhappy stay in England, and with the subsiding of the volcano on its home island, the Tristan colony decided to go home again, and the population was repatriated to its remote location in the South Atlantic Ocean. So remote is Tristan da Cunha, that it is known as the most isolated inhabited place on the globe. Outside the Tristan community, the nearest inhabitant is more than one thousand miles away, on the coast of Africa.

For a generation the information about Tristan's population having a propensity for asthma was no more than a curiosity. But in 1990, researchers in Canada and the United States started thinking about causes of asthma, especially the possibility that asthma might be a genetic disease and perhaps the gene which caused asthma might be located.

There was no better place to find an asthma gene or genes than on Tristan da Cunha. But the islanders hadn't forgotten the treatment they had received at the hands of science thirty years before. It took a couple of years of delicate negotiations before two researchers were allowed to go to Tristan, spend several months there, and take blood samples from virtually every person living on the island.

The researchers then returned to North America with the samples and began the arduous work of trying to isolate the gene associated with asthma. The first of those genes was discovered in 1997 and 1998.

Eventually, by 2003, researchers found all the asthma linked genes. Then came the struggle to figure out how those genes were related and what they did.

"Mother Nature is very, very smart," the Guide said with a smile. "She plays by very precise rules. The only problem mankind has is trying to figure out what those rules are and how to play with them."

For instance, one of the genes that triggers asthma attacks was discovered in 2002, but researchers took seven years to figure out how to turn that gene on and off. Some scientists were looking for chemical switches—so they could give someone a drug which would control the genetic switch; others were trying to determine if they could replace the defective gene with a properly working one.

By 2012, the answers were in place, and it turned out that a vaccine was the best form of asthma control. In 2018, the first group of babies were given the asthma vaccine; it became universal treatment by 2022.

"And that," said the Guide, "is how Napoleon defeated asthma by leaving Elba."

My mouth was agape listening to the incredible tale. "What a string of coincidences. If Napoleon had stayed put; if he hadn't been exiled to St. Helena, if . . ."

"That, Shawn, is why I've told you a dozen times that nothing is written in stone. It can take any number of events to lead down one path. And steps off that path can change everything.

"Don't let these obstacles deter you from telling the world about what is going to happen. Perhaps just the telling can set good deeds in motion or prevent bad deeds from being executed. You can't be concerned about that. You must give the message and let the rest of the world believe it, disbelieve it, act on it, or ignore it. It's up to them, not to you."

The years between 2005 and 2050 were filled with al-most yearly discoveries of genes that control or fail to con-trol killer diseases—the cause of multiple sclerosis; the mutation that caused muscular dystrophy; the series of genes that misfire and cause insulin-producing cells to shut down, causing diabetes.

With the discovery of the gene and new ways of repair-ing these genes or replacing them, science began to win the battle of keeping people healthy.

But despite the promise of health, the illusion of beauty seemed more important to people and, therefore, to inves-tors. Even before the p53 gene's mysteries were unraveled, the corruption of genetics had already taken root.

In 2003, a researcher discovered what gene controlled eye color. Industry bought up the man's discoveries and bid billions for his patent on his follow-up work that showed how to insert a gene for eye color into a fetus. Immediately there was a clamoring for babies with blue eyes, until a movie star in 2010, with the most vivid blue-green eyes, took Hollywood by storm, and created a gen-eration of lagoon green-eyed children. When the actress died in 2068—in childbirth at age seventy-three—the au-topsy revealed that those trademark blue-green eyes were the result, not of fortunate genetics, but of skillful use of contact lenses.

The discovery of the gene which coded for hair color almost caused worldwide riots. The scientist who came up with that information found himself worth billions, until he was assassinated by the father of a failed beauty queen con-testant who lost to a contestant with a more perfect shade of auburn—considered to be the hair color of choice in 2015.

It was in early 2013 that a clandestine group of scientists, multibillionaires, and some genuinely disturbed, but wealthy, people met to create the Clone People—an attempt to create perfect people who would live in a perfect world run by a perfect government.

The first order of business was for the group to move to Wyoming, north of Devils Tower, and start buying up land, acres and acres of land. Each of the twelve hundred members of the Family, as they called themselves, were assigned to amass as much land as possible in northern Crook County, where there were few people—and fewer every year; little industry—declining even faster than the population, and little interest from the county seat fifty miles away. The land was purchased through intermediaries by tough negotiators who were told to get the land at any price, but never to allow the local people to realize there was a concerted effort under way to put together a fifty-square-mile enterprise that would be the seat of power for the new Family Order.

It took ten years to put together the land holdings and another dozen or so to establish a community, complete with schools, telecommunications, businesses, and, most importantly, a state-of-the-art medical center equipped with the best genetics laboratory money could buy. The staff was already in place: Gene scientists who could create new DNA strings in the laboratory; genetic fetalogists who could remove cells from a developing fetus in the womb, determine their structure, and make alterations and additions before infecting the fetus with a virus which changed the gene structure.

By the middle of the twenty-first century, dozens of Perfect Children were appearing on the prairies and hills around Devils Tower. The preponderance of auburn-haired, green-eyed children with genetically engineered height and shapes wouldn't be noticed for a number of years, and by the time the work of the Cloningers came to light, the perfect society they created was already spiraling into oblivion—having created absolutely no lasting impression on society.

The incredible problem with the Cloningers was that their goal—to produce perfect children, with perfect teeth, noses, hair and eye color—was achieved. Indeed the careful laboratory work managed to create a bunch of children who looked so much alike that parents sometimes had a hard time telling their children from their neighbors'.

Unfortunately that was the problem. The Cloningers set out to be a perfect society, and as a perfect society there was a desire that all ethnic groups be involved. There were professional African-Americans—and only a couple were professional athletes; there were professional European-Americans—and only a few of them earned their income from sports; there were professional Hispanics and professional Asian-Americans—and only a few of them were mathematicians.

The best and the brightest of the races contributed their monies, their ideals, and their hopes to create something different and wonderful in isolated Wyoming. They should have realized—and evidence was apparent that many of the principals were aware—that if they had to perform all their business in secret, behind closed doors, that there was something basically wrong and undemocratic about what was happening in the shadow of Devils Tower.

"You can't fool with Mother Nature—most of the time," the Guide said, before continuing his history lesson in my mind.

It took months of negotiating before everyone agreed on the shape of the faces of the children—they had found the genes which controlled those functions; they decided not to mess with skin color, although those genes were located, described, and shown to be manipulatable as early as 2011. There was general agreement on hair color and eye color and on how many babies the colony could handle. Actually, there were no limits on children. The area and the incomes of the colony members were large enough to take care of virtually any number of children the membership could produce—and even though it took nine full months to develop a child from conception to full term, scientists figured out a way to shorten the length of time a woman had to carry the child.

"Wait a minute," I said to the Guide, and almost instantly the classroom scene dissolved and I was in my bed back in Greenwich Village. The Guide was sitting in the overstuffed chair, the *New York Times* opened to the crossword puzzle. He had a pencil in one hand, the television remote control in the other. The television was scanning through the channels.

I watched, my brain in numb mode, as the Comedy Channel, public access, NBC and seventy-five other attempts at entertainment or news flashed across the screen.

I shook my head to try to remember what I was trying to think of, and the thoughts returned to me. "What do you mean we found a way to shorten the time it takes to carry a child?"

"Very simple. You discover that it's detrimental to a woman's health to carry a baby to term," he said, scribbling something into the puzzle boxes. "About 2020, it became common practice."

And we left my room. I looked at the Guide, now dressed in a surgical gown, a white mask covering his face. I realized I was wearing a mask as well and stood alongside nurses and doctors in an operating theater.

"Uh, why are we dressed like this? No one can see us."

The Guide put his finger to his lips and whispered. He pointed to the patient. "She's slightly sedated," he said, "and in that condition she might be able to discern us psychically. She's in a trancelike condition, much the way you are when you see me."

Like I am now, I thought, trying to understand how I can be in a trance and conjure up the Guide and yet discuss the conditions of the trance while in a trance. *Oh, hell*, I said to myself, *I'll explore that later.*

The Guide continued to talk in a whisper, his voice barely detectable over the hubbub in the operating room. The surgeon was making an incision in the woman's swollen abdomen with a laserlike knife. "That's a handheld light scalpel," the Guide said. "As sharp as a razor, yet it can be self-suturing, literally fusing the skin together. In the right hands—those of any capable and experienced surgeon—there won't even be a scar."

"The woman is undergoing preterm fetal removal. The fetus is surgically removed from the uterus and then placed in a bath of fluid, closely resembling amniotic fluid, where the fetus spends the rest of its prenatal life.

"By the year 2000, you would have thought that in industrialized, advanced societies, infant mortality would be at historically low levels," the Guide said as the medical team removed the tiny grayish fetus—I could see that this child-to-be was a girl—from the womb.

But, he said, paradoxically, infant mortality leveled off and refused to drop no matter what the socioeconomic status of the child and the child's mother was. In 2001, a major study was undertaken by one of the branches of the National Institutes of Health to try and find out what was causing babies to die or fail to thrive.

It took five years of study and analysis before it became apparent what was going on. Quite simply, the children that failed to survive infancy failed to survive because of the actions, reactions, or inaction of their mothers.

A small fraction of mothers were so devastated by the process of pregnancy and birth—postpartum depression—that children became victims. Some children were abandoned physically; others were abandoned psychologically. Researchers at the Harvard Medical School were able to demonstrate unequivocally that some mothers who suffered from depression after the birth of a child could make their depression "contagious," affecting their infants even when the babies were just a couple of months old.

By 2009, numerous studies and reports in respected journals determined that the eighth and ninth months of pregnancy were the riskiest for the child and for the mother—not exactly news to millions of mothers. In 2011, a prestigious group of child psychiatrists, noting the dangers of the last eight weeks of pregnancy, proposed that women should not give birth, but should have the children taken from the womb and developed in special baths which mimicked the placenta.

The idea was assaulted on ethical, legal, and religious levels, but medical and psychological experts began a thoughtful assessment of what the researchers were saying.

1. Removing the child from the womb after seven months would prevent harm to the mother and child. Most cases of high blood pressure, gestational diabetes, weight gain, swelling in the legs, etc., occurred during the last two months of pregnancy. Advice to eat right and exercise, the hallmarks of good health and good pregnancies, had as much impact on mothers in the early twenty-first cen-

tury as it had had on mothers in the previous one hundred years of industrialized life.

2. Transmission of life-threatening or physically threatening diseases—the transmission of AIDS, the complications of herpes—could be attenuated.

3. Given the rising numbers of single women having children, the need for these women to leave work near the end of pregnancy resulted in nutritional deficits to children. Mothers who had limited funds or limited transportation sometimes—in truth, frequently—didn't eat properly and sometimes drank destructively. By removal of the fetus in the eighth month, optimal nutrition would be obtained.

4. Birth canal trauma to the child and to the mothers would be eliminated.

5. Childbirth pain would be eliminated.

6. Postpartum depression could be anticipated, treated vigorously, and controlled before the baby rejoined the mother at home, reducing the risk of psychological harm.

7. The mother would have time to get back into "shape"—a shape not nearly so changed as by full-term pregnancy—physically, emotionally, and financially. She would also have time to locate and set up support teams, such as nannies or willing relatives before the child came home, and to get back to full steam at work—providing another psychologically enriching experience for the mother which would be refocused on the child.

It took a few years of arguments and a number of horrific instances of mothers who killed or injured babies, before the arguments of the psychologists became persuasive to the public.

Even so, the technology to create the new system wasn't ready for another decade.

But by 2030, virtually no babies were allowed to be delivered at term.

As the Guide droned on, I watched in amazement as the fetus was lifted from the mother, carried to a tank of water, then immersed in the bath. *My God*, I thought, *the baby is going to drown*.

The Guide shook his head. ''When the baby is in the womb it breathes amniotic fluid that contains oxygen. That's the fluid in those baths. Similar fluids are available right now on Earth. In fact, it was demonstrated in some movie a few years ago.''

I actually remembered the movie, a science-fiction thriller called *The Abyss*, better known for its daring special effects than for plot, acting, or scientific substance. But I remembered that scene in the movie and the comment that ''the lungs remember'' how to breathe oxygen from fluid.

Nurses wheeled the fetus into another room. Meanwhile, doctors using the light scalpel finished closing the abdominal incision. Only a faint red line, maybe an eighth of an inch thick, remained on the skin. A doctor told the patient, ''In a couple of weeks that will fade away, too. See, you can barely see the other mark made when we did the twins.'' The mother smiled wanly.

The fetus was placed in the prenatal placental incubator. Various tubes fed oxygen, nutrients, and other chemicals that would give the baby strong bones and healthy teeth, and would protect it against dozens of childhood and adult illnesses, including the dreaded Helicobacter pylori bug found to be responsible for ulcers, gastritis, and even several forms of gastrointestinal cancer.

By the time the child was removed from the liquid baths, he or she had developed to such a point that each was likely to sleep through the night the first night at home from the birthing centers. A sleeping baby was a quiet child, and child abuse incidents dropped like a stone on the statistical charts.

Instances of postpartum depression were virtually eliminated, follow-up studies in 2040 determined. The procedure was overwhelmingly successful, and, aside from accident, infant mortality vanished from nations sophisticated enough and rich enough to have the medical facilities needed to create the system.

Almost a second later, I was back in that Wyoming classroom, looking at all those similar children, and I still didn't follow the algebra lesson.

The Guide continued his dissertation on how babies were birthed in the twenty-first century. "One of the major impacts of the system was that it gave the Cloningers the opportunity to have more and more babies. Instead of taking nine months to have a child and then another six weeks to two months before a woman was physically ready to try pregnancy again—about a one year time frame. Now Cloninger women were ready for another pregnancy eight months after the first pregnancy. Do the math, Shawn," he said. "Three babies in two years; six in four years; twelve in eight years. Hundreds of babies; all perfect."

And like all perfect plans, destined to collapse.

The first wave of babies born to the Cloningers were loved as any babies would be. The trouble came from the in-laws. While many relatives couldn't understand why Jack and Jill would leave Brooklyn and take up residence in Wyoming, that in itself wasn't a reason for crisis.

But when, for example Angelo Russo and his wife, the former Maria Nicoletti, returned to Franklin Square, Long Island, with Angelo, Jr., the Russos went into shock, and the Nicolettis worried about how long it would take for their daughter to be killed by the in-laws. Little Angelo Jr., not only didn't have his dad's solid jaw, Roman nose, and heaps of dark brown hair, Angelo, Jr., didn't have his father's brown eyes—the same exact color as his mother's eyes. In fact, Angelo had wispy curls of platinum blond and the fiercest turquoise eyes in the world.

The family tried vainly for hours trying to figure out whom the child looked like and came to the decision that he certainly didn't look like his father, so he must look like the milkman. The stay in Brooklyn for the baptism was strained, discourteous, hostile, and truncated. The younger Russos swore never to return to the homes of their parents, who were certain that Maria, despite her angelic name, was some kind of adulteress, and burly Angelo a knowing cuckold. When the only contact came in the form of new pictures of additional children, churned out like clockwork faster than nature could have provided, and the children still didn't look like the parents, the strained relationships became chasms.

The reaction of relatives to the various children that spilled out of Wyoming for the next several years was similar among the African-Americans, the Asian-Americans, and others.

Now the Cloningers, who couldn't explain to their own relatives why their children looked so different, found that their isolation was real and wasn't of their own doing. They were being shunned for having perfect children. It didn't take long for the beginnings of the Abandonments. The perfect children from the perfect community were being set adrift; sent to orphanages; sent away to boarding school and then to summer camp and then to college without ever returning home; without ever seeing their parents again.

In some cases, by the time the children were graduated from college, they could no longer locate their parents, who had moved away from Crook County and had begun new families—this time without help from the genetic engineers and without forwarding addresses. What was left of the Cloningers perfect world turned into dust towns or isolated ranches where a handful of people met to discuss the promise that was never fulfilled. By 2060, the Cloninger experiment was history.

Many scores of Cloninger children who were raised well financially, grew up without knowledge of family; without focus; without a rudder in the sea of life. Most of them became successful in whatever fields they drifted into—after all, most studies have shown that looks always play a bigger role in getting started than do brains.

Many other Cloningers, however, were lost souls desperately reaching out for a firm hand—and that included Nabyla's wife.

4

THE HEROINE BAGS HER
GAME LIGHT-YEARS AWAY

REDMOND, NABYLA THOUGHT. WHAT A STRANGE NAME, for such a great-looking guy.

"Redmond," she snapped, and the waiter turned smartly toward her. Nabyla had already finished her salad and coffee but the young man intrigued her, especially those piercing blue-green eyes. She was pleased that the rooftop restaurant in Greater Albany had one of those quaint twentieth-century distinctions of having waiters introduce themselves by first name.

Redmond, all six-foot-four with nearly perfect features—he reminded Nabyla of the terrific character actor Hugh Grant, who was still doing romantic comedy in his nineties, stood poised before her, his electronic stylus in hand. She stared into his eyes; he stared back and finally dropped his gaze, as if suddenly afraid someone had discovered a deep, dark secret.

Nabyla was embarrassed for him. "Er, what do you recommend for dessert?" she said. His pleasant smile returned, and Nabyla felt her heart melt. He ran down a list of exotic pies and cheesecakes.

31

"Key lime pie?" Nabyla questioned. "In Albany? In January?"

"Well, it's on the list of desserts," Redmond said without a lot of certainty in his voice.

"What color is it?"

"Green." He smiled, trapped.

"Hah, I knew it. You can't get real Key lime pie in New York."

"You know that since the blight struck Florida in '57, it's been nearly impossible to get any real Key limes anywhere. I don't know why they keep this on the list. I think the cappuccino cheesecake is the best dessert we have," the waiter said. Nabyla guessed his age as twenty-two to twenty-five, which would make him perfect for her. She checked for rings, although she realized that his being ringless meant little in the society of 2088. His fingers were bare.

Nabyla leaned back in her chair and gazed up at the cloudless sky. The sun blazed down and warmed her face. The pseudoglass dome, designed originally for nursing homes, allowed enough ultraviolet light through the glass to activate cells which began the chemical cascade in the body that creates vitamin D. In Albany in the winter no one went outside—it was eighteen below zero on the Fahrenheit scale, Americans being the last holdouts against universal use of Celsius gauges.

She stretched her arms in back of her head, mainly to give Redmond a good view of her well-maintained and much-admired body, wrapped tightly in the newest wool-like sweater. "I dunno," Nabyla said. "Cheesecake is loaded with calories and fat."

She was fishing for compliments, and Redmond knew it. "I don't think you have much to worry about on that score," he said quietly. Nabyla brightened and ordered the cheesecake.

She returned the next day and the day after, when she had a break from training. After the fourth lunch, Redmond finally suggested a date after work. Three months later they were married.

A flashing light roused Nabyla from her musings. The

cold, wintry nights in the cabin near Lake Lucerne faded
out of her mind instantly. The flashing light on the heads-
up display meant that her sonar had detected movement of
objects that traveled at humanoid speed and fit into the
proper size she had programmed into the computer. She
checked the weapon readout for the hundredth time. Even
through the scope of the rifle, Nabyla could not see anything. The computer detector aimed her rifle toward the
dark path.

Nabyla looked around. The winged creatures that were
so efficient at killing had all but disappeared from the sky.
The first sun had already set, the second was nearing the
horizon. *Hmm, the birds sleep at night*, she said to herself,
*and that's when the humanoids come out to hunt and scav-
enge*.

She clenched her back teeth and immediately heard Davis's voice. "What's up?"

"I think it's time. Begin your descent to the area
marked."

It would take twenty to thirty minutes for Davis to swoop
in. Nabyla figured it would take five to ten minutes before
her target emerged and was dropped. Then she had to protect her catch until Davis showed.

The male appeared at the end of the path. Nabyla locked
him in the sights of the rifle. His computer image was
stored in the rifle computer, which would focus on him until
Nabyla squeezed the trigger or aborted the contact. Slowly
Nabyla dropped the binoculars from her forehead to her
eyes. The creature seemed to be looking directly at her, but
there was no way he could see her. He peered at the sky,
scanning from left to right. He took two cautious steps and
froze, again scanning the sky. He repeated the action three
more times, and was now about fifteen feet from the forest
path. Another form emerged at the edge, smaller and defi-
nitely female, its breasts clearly visible. Both were clad in
loincloths.

Nabyla was about to squeeze the trigger when another
form appeared at the path, a smaller form, obviously a
child, perhaps five or six years old. The female held out
her hand like a traffic cop, and the child froze. Nabyla

checked the time: Davis was still eleven minutes away. The
male moved off to the right; the female to the left. Nabyla
could see some form of weapon in their hands. She punched
the computer and the heads-up display revealed a clear sky
and several creatures on the surface. They were either too
far from the humanoids to see them, or they weren't interested. The child moved slowly up behind the adults, so the
humanoids formed a triangle.

Nabyla considered her choices and executed her first
strike. The sound was suppressed by high-technology baf-
fles, and the tranquilizing dart was on its way toward the
male figure. Even before it hit him, Nabyla had locked onto
the child. She knew that when the man dropped the female
would immediately flee to the forest coverage. But she also
thought that if these humanoids were as human as they
looked, the female wouldn't leave without the child.

The male suddenly clutched his side. He must have
yelled or made a startling sound because the female instantly bolted toward the path. The child, however, started
toward the fallen male, only halting when the female yelled
at it. The child stopped, turned to follow the female, and
then screamed and grabbed his neck where Nabyla's second
dart had hit him. The woman froze and nearly stumbled.
She had only seconds to decide whether to reach safety or
aid the child. She hesitated, and Nabyla's third dart struck
her in the right thigh. She muffled her cry and collapsed to
the ground.

The cries of pain had brought a reaction from the varied
creatures on the plain, whose heads picked up immediately.
Dozens of critters began a rapid run toward the cries. Nabyla took up her laser-guided assault rifle and blasted the
lead animals into bloody pulp. The followers halted and
began to feed on the remains.

The hungry creatures didn't even look up as Davis
swooped down to the site, greeted by Nabyla, who had
driven her scooter from the blind to the spot where the three
aliens lay unconscious. It took five minutes to bundle the
aliens onto Davis's craft, load the scooter, and take off.

Nabyla checked her catch. All were unconscious but
breathing normally. All of them looked amazingly like people on Earth.

5

THE GENE RIOTS ERUPT AND BURN THE INSURANCE CITY

"HELLO."

"Ed, it's Shawn." I tried to control the quiver in my voice, but I failed.

"What's wrong?"

"I had another really bad dream. Really disturbing. I'm really upset."

"You certainly sound upset. Was it too much coriander at the Indian restaurant? Or are we talking psychic revelations again?"

With Ed you can never be sure if he's kidding around; if he's being insensitive; if he's just plain bored, tired, or pressed for time; or if he's being a mean son of a bitch. That's the problem with Aquarians, you can never tell if they are being aloof because of their nature or because they are trying to prove something to themselves or to others.

"I think . . . it was the Guide, again. I think there was a new message, and it really frightened me."

"Tell me about it," he said, his voice softer and more focused. He was paying attention. I dismissed those nasty thoughts and repeated Ed's favorite expression to myself. He said it came from too many years as a street-level reporter: "Just because I'm paranoid, Shawn, it doesn't mean people aren't out to get me."

I took a couple of breaths. "I was dreaming—"

"Shawn," he interrupted, "were you really dreaming, or do you just think you were dreaming? What were you doing when you had the dream? Think back. What were you doing before you called me? About what time was it? Relax and tell what you saw."

Body odor. A wretched, bitter, acrid smell that leaped at me as I walked past the bank's gated and locked doorway. There, sitting on the ground, knees bent, feet on the concrete, was the man, a bottle wrapped in a brown paper bag in his right hand, a cigarette smoldering between the fingers on his left hand. A baseball cap with the barely discernible logo of the Pittsburgh Pirates was pulled down to protect his eyes from the overcast sky.

For some reason he looked up at me as I passed by; the deep wrinkles around his eyes, however, failed to hide his piercing green eyes. I felt a tremor in my body and my feet felt light. His face was striking, handsome, almost gorgeous. I knew the facts of life: good-looking men do better than average Joes. *This person must have had better chances than most*, I thought. *Why is he homeless, reeking, drunk, and destitute?*

Before I could answer, I found myself standing in a crowd on the corner of a street. Police were standing behind barricades, absentmindedly slapping nightsticks into their palms. Across the road, firemen scurried with hoses toward the tall structure enveloped in flames. Glass windows exploded from heat and shattered into millions of shards, which rained down on the firemen, who ducked under whatever protection was available.

I searched for the Guide, knowing instinctively that he had something to do with what I was watching. I found him a couple of feet away, peering intently into the inferno.

"Insurance company," he said. "It's the Gene Riots of '23."

It was far easier for medical science and geneticists to

find genes that didn't work right or that caused problems in the body than it was for science to figure out what to do about it.

The first thought was that by finding out who was susceptible to a disease—say lung cancer, it would be the doctor's job to tell the person involved: "Hey, you see this gene here—blown up about ten thousand times with an electron microscope—that gene isn't going to work right when you start sucking down nicotine, tars, and a thousand other chemicals that Brown & Williamson and other manufacturers are putting in cigarettes. So don't even think about starting to smoke. This gene and those ingredients will kill you dead as a doornail."

The Guide added, "I'm just taking poetic license here, you understand."

I nodded, but said, "Are we still going to have cigarettes in the future at all? I thought we were doing fairly well on the way to a smokeless society by 2000."

"Actually, it seems that geneticists saved what was left of the tobacco companies in the United States in 2019, when the lung cancer gene was isolated. This was the gene which, if a person inherited it, gave them a two-in-three chance of developing cancer caused by cigarette-type smoke. But it turned out that only about thirty-eight percent of the population have this gene abnormality. So if you wanted to smoke, you could take a genetic test and determine if you were at risk. If you weren't, then it was safe to smoke. At least you wouldn't get cancer. Emphysema was another problem; heart disease also. But cancer has always been the motivating force behind the urge to quit smoking. And if you were protected against cigarette smoke, and you liked smoking . . ."

"You digress," I said.

"I digress," the Guide agreed.

By 2015, so many disease genes had been identified that a decent, extensive genetic test could determine who was likely to develop diseases as common as breast cancer to relatively uncommon illnesses such as retinoblastoma—a cancer of the developing cells in the eyes, often causing blindness, if not death, in babies.

The problem for people getting these tests was that while science could tell you what was likely to befall you as you grew older, science couldn't do much about it other than to warn you to get prophylactic treatment. Obviously if you had a lung cancer susceptibility, you wouldn't smoke; if you had a susceptibility for diabetes, you had to watch your weight, etc.

"Genetic researchers were quick to tell the public that knowing they had these bad genes was wonderful news because they would have the power to deal with the future—and they'd know what they would be passing on to other generations. But there was a flip side to knowledge, and the flip side is evil," he said.

Maybe the Cloningers were evil people by wanting to create perfect people, but whatever was in their minds was nothing compared to what happened in the insurance world.

By 2020, an alarming trend was turning up. More and more young, bright college graduates were going to apply for jobs with prestigious companies and were being turned down for employment. One man from Tennessee, a Vanderbilt graduate, was turned down for one law office job after another. He had passed the bar; had terrific grades in college; was highly presentable; and always received the top marks in interviews—but he never got a job.

He finally opened his own office, and because of his special skills created a name for himself in Nashville representing country and western singers. It took only a few months before he had to hire a couple of secretaries, some paralegals, and started looking for associates.

As he started adding personnel, he realized he needed to offer benefits for his workers, including health insurance. He sent the employees to have physicals, and nothing was amiss until he tried to include himself in the coverage. In a foul-up that was going to create shock waves for a decade, a clerk at the insurance company sent a notice to the law firm saying that the lawyer mentioned was uninsurable because of genetic tests taken at birth that showed he was likely to develop Lou Gehrig's disease.

The lawyer was stunned; but more than that he was angry. He realized that this genetic information was what was keeping him from being hired by other law firms. The would-be employers found out that he was uninsurable and would have had to pay extreme premiums to cover him.

The lawyer was angry because federal laws were developed in the 1990s to prevent anyone from being denied coverage on the basis of genetic testing. It was obvious that not only was there a clandestine effort to subvert that ruling, but that the nation's largest insurance companies were working in concert to prevent health insurance coverage from being given to people most likely to need the coverage.

"It's a great way to gamble," the Guide said. "Simply know who the losers are and don't bet on them."

The lawyer began a campaign to find out how many other people had been denied insurance and, therefore, jobs, and had their lives, careers, and happiness destroyed by insurance-company abuse of genetic knowledge. He led a march of more than three hundred thousand people from Washington, D.C., to Hartford, Connecticut, the nominal Insurance Capital of the U.S., to protest the insurance-company actions and to demand reparations to those who had been injured in the dirty war perpetrated on the people by the insurers.

The gathering in downtown Hartford in the spring of 2023, however, got out of control. Mobs of people attacked one of the glossier symbols of the industry and set it ablaze.

"The stench you smelled from that bum was the smell of future shenanigans," the Guide said.

The Gene Riots of '23 failed to win damages for the people affected—it turned out that so many millions had been denied coverage that repayment involved numbers too big even for the insurers to repay.

But the idea of government-paid health care, delayed, derailed, and moribund since the days of Bill Clinton, was quickly dusted off. While few were willing to put a lot of faith in the government to act fairly toward those who were genetically challenged, it was now obvious that industries could not be trusted not to stack the deck by using genetic information to protect themselves against monetary losses.

In 2025, insurance companies were prohibited from writing any form of health insurance, even special lines of coverage meant for high rollers.

"Genes, Shawn, genes. Genes are everything that is now and will be in the future," the Guide said. "Our travels will bring us back to genetics time and time again because genetics and the future of the world are tied together—for better or for worse.

"The more we understand genes, the more we will understand ourselves. The more we understand ourselves and the world around us, the more we are going to be able to make changes that may benefit mankind or destroy it.

"Genes will play a recurring and important role in our travels and in one path to the future which you will be seeing, discussing, and telling the world. The people of the world need to know where we are going and how we are going to get there."

His words impressed me, but I wondered, *Is anyone going to listen?*

6

THREE ALIENS TO
THE BASE SHIP

DAVIS WAS SHORT AND STOCKY. ON EARTH HE WOULD have weighed 225. Some people might have considered him overweight, but Davis was all muscle. *And especially the area between his ears,* Nabyla said to herself.

But as with everyone else in her crew, Davis was someone she had to get along with, just as everyone else had to get along with her. The psychological makeup of a space crew was a delicate organism. If there was something about someone that you didn't like, being together for ten to twenty years wasn't going to make those foibles any less annoying.

Davis was simply a foul-mouthed, biased jerk, who also happened to be one of the best pilots Nabyla had ever known. She'd seen Davis maneuver around speeding asteroids with the confidence and skill of a motorcyclist zipping through a freeway traffic jam. Davis was utterly fearless, yet he never even came close to putting himself or a member of his crew in danger. "Anyone can avoid an accident," Davis said. "All you need are good reflexes, a good vehicle, and a little bit of warning. Real skill is never getting to the point where an accident is imminent.''

It was probably the most profound statement Davis ever made, Nablya thought. But he was true to his credo. Davis always had things under control when he was flying. The one thing he could never control was his mouth.

Davis stood over Nabyla, the automated pilot streaking above the planet surface. ''It'll be about ten minutes before we are ready to translate to orbit,'' he said. ''I don't think we have to worry about finding another aircraft here unless those bird-thingamajigs fly a lot higher that I've seen.''

Nabyla was securing the legs of the child with the duct tape she'd taken from the main ship's storage tank. The arms and legs of the female and male humanoids had been taped together; a rope tied them snugly to the backs of the crew chairs.

''Think they'll take the jolt to space, OK?'' Davis asked.

''I'm more concerned about them throwing up in zero grav,'' Nabyla said.

''Maybe they'll sleep 'til then,'' Davis said. ''How much juice did you hit them with?''

''I figured them for sixty kilos.'' She pointed to the male. ''That's about right for him. He should be dull for another hour. She's going to be out for a longer time. I'm concerned that the child might not make it.''

Davis read her thoughts. If the child died, someone was going to find out about it eventually. Sooner or later scientists would analyze the creatures' language, and they'd discover the child was missing. He went over to the child, a boy, and felt for a pulse by picking up the boy's wrist.

Nabyla snorted. ''You think they've got a pulse in the same place as us?''

Davis glanced up at her. ''This one does. It seems pretty steady. You know, Nablya, these''—he gestured at the humanoids—''really look like people, aside from the skin. I haven't seen too many green humans.''

''When we get to the ship, we'll put them in the brig. They won't be able to hurt themselves there, and we can monitor them before we put them in the bath,'' Nabyla said.

''Ooh, they are not gonna like that, I'll bet. Your wife still hates it.''

Nabyla could feel her body tense. She would have given Davis a forearm to the bridge of his nose if she had thought it would do any good. It had been decades since the slur was used in proper company, and it was incredibly poor taste for a subordinate crew member to refer to a captain's spouse in that manner.

Nabyla was raised long after the description had been dropped from use in polite company and long after the U.S. government had adopted the Poor Language Act of 2066, in which researchers spelled out in detail why certain words were offensive to various groups. The act didn't ban the use of the words from radio, television, or the Internet but only from use in federal documents. It was a rather fluid document in that various ethnic groups often grew tired of being referred to in a certain manner and decided they would rather be associated with a different adjective.

But one slur that remained on the list without change over the years was "wife." At one time, a wife was the female partner of a man, and in pre-twenty-first-century society the wife was supposed to raise children, keep the house neat, cook food, and comfort the male partner sexually when requested.

By the end of the twentieth century, however, the roles of men and women were becoming blurred. There were no fields—save most professional sports—that excluded women, and often the woman became the main breadwinner in the home. Numerous television shows and movies in the early twenty-first century portrayed the new American family as a woman who went to work and came home to a sparkling clean home and a loving husband.

In one such show in 2007, the husband, who in addition to taking the kids to school and preparing dinner, was also a semisuccessful writer, complained to his successful lawyer spouse about how much work he was doing at home. She replied, "What you need is a wife." It drew laughs then but actually became a rallying cry for millions of women who called the term "wife" a demeaning description. "A wife is just a maid that stays the night" the more radical of the women said to newspaper editors, politicians, and others who used the term in public statements. With more and more men accepting the home as their choice of occupation, and with women being freed from requiring long recuperation after birth thanks to changes in childbirth, the insulting slur often was directed at men. Since most women hated the term, and burgeoning groups of men were now feeling the sting of the comment, the usage slipped from polite company.

Eventually the nation understood that "wife" was as demeaning a slur as calling someone by a racial or religious epithet. Of course, it's easy to ban something in public, but not in private. And Davis, who was born after the Poor Language Act had been enacted, still used it in his everyday speech. Nabyla could only assume he picked it up from his Neandertal parents or Stone Age friends.

Nabyla scanned the small runabout's cockpit, still satisfied that the captive humanoids were secure, and waited for Davis to jolt them into space and rendezvous with their orbiting ship. She eyed Davis and thought, *Well, maybe he is a boor, but there isn't any machine with an engine or wings that he can't fly.* "Besides," she mumbled under her breath, "none of us are perfect, least of all me."

We rose together as if I were holding on to Superman's arm. I barely glanced behind as Earth fell away and the warmth of the sun receded. At one point I remember wondering how I managed to get outside. One moment I was sitting on my sofa talking to the Guide, and the next moment we were traveling in outer space.

I know enough science to realize that if I were really in outer space, I would have died from lack of oxygen. We sped through the Solar System. I thought I recognized Mars with the network of rilles that once were thought to be canals. I could distinguish the vast shape of Jupiter in the distance, its Red Eye swirling malevolently, staring at me evilly.

Abruptly we stopped and hung silently in the void, dark and quiet. Slowly I became aware of huge dark shapes floating in the heavens. I studied the shapes as they twisted and tumbled and quickly recognized them as chunks of stone—asteroids of various sizes and shapes. The ones I was looking at were too small to be seen even with powerful Moon-based telescopes of the twenty-first century.

"The telescopes were the first government/commercial enterprise on the Moon," the Guide explained. The reexploration of the Moon, he explained, began as a worldwide cooperative project in 2008. World governments, the U.S., Russia, Europe, China, and Japan in particular, pooled resources to begin regular scientific expeditions to the surface of the Moon.

The decision to go for a Moon-based project reflected visionary thinking on the part of scientists, government, and industry. The space station-based complex would be handy for growing crystals and computer parts in a gravity-free environment, but space travel and space exploration—the true future of mankind—would require a land-based colony that had available resources. The Moon had resources; the space station had to have resources brought to it.

The impetus to get humanity off its own planet, however, came only with the catastrophe of the collision in space between the moons of Jupiter in 2021 and the subsequent deadly asteroid showers that threatened to destroy Earth. Moon-based telescopes aimed at locating wayward asteroids were the first successful commercial application of the Moon colonies. The first permanent habitation of the Moon began in 2048 when the United Nations authorized the occupation of a temporary dome on the Moon by a permanent civilian population. The first colony consisted of about twenty-five families, all connected in some manner to the operation of the telescopes.

In 2051, another colony, dedicated to mining operations on the Moon and the receipt of mineral-rich asteroids, was established about fifty miles away. It was a smaller colony at the start but soon outgrew the first settlement.

By 2053, government operation of the telescopes was turned over to private industries, which bid to develop and run the system. The aim was to locate the largest of the asteroids, map them, round them up with asteroid cowboys, and herd the rocks back to the Moon, where they could be mined.

In 2060, the first metal fabricating plant went on-line on

the Moon's surface. The power for the plant was supplied by solar energy, captured by lunar satellites which were able to refocus the sun's energy to collectors on the Moon's surface with a great deal more efficiency than the solar energy systems being used by Earth. On the Moon there was no atmosphere to interfere with the beams of sun energy; while on Earth, a hurricane or sandstorm could diminish the amount of energy produced to barely usable levels.

The Moon-based fabrications of airtight containers now allowed the asteroid cowboys the chance to actually live comfortably in space. It meant they weren't confined to small four-person craft. There could actually be minicolonies floating in space that would be large enough to handle supplies that could last for a couple of years or more.

It also meant that the boxcar-sized prefabricated habitats, made of metals hard enough to deflect all but the largest of meteors and meteorites, could be towed to other planets, where they would become temporary structures. In 2070, the first of these structures was placed on Mars, beginning the colonization of that planet.

By 2075, the system was creating work for tens of thousands of Moon-based citizens and for thousands more who lived in minor colonies on Mars and the stable moons of Jupiter. The development of those minor colonies took a lot of pressure off the burgeoning development of the Moon, which now began to settle into a second form of development—as a tourist attraction and destination.

In the 2080s hundreds of people would arrive on special shuttlecraft from Earth, stay at the Sheraton Luna, and then travel around the Moon, climbing mountains, exploring caves, and taking awe-inspiring pictures of Earth. Most of the visitors as well as those who lived on the Moon frequently interrupted their conversations to ask themselves why exploration of the Moon had been so shortsightedly aborted during the twentieth century.

"The conquest of space could have begun thirty years sooner," the Guide said, "but after Americans reached the Moon in 1969 and made a few more trips there through 1972, the desire to get into space was torpedoed by the

United States involvement in Vietnam. The U.S. could either fight an ill-advised war and spend billions trying to protect South Vietnam from communism or it could spend billions developing a coherent space program. War won.''

The United States space program that took it to the Moon was a gimmick approach. The Soviet Union was first in space with a man-made satellite; first in space with a live object; first to have a man orbit the Earth. With the U.S.'s scientific manhood at stake, President John F. Kennedy pointed toward the Moon and made it the goal of the space program.

U.S. technology got the country to the Moon first. It was an enormous technical, scientific, and human accomplishment. Eventually, six different two-man teams walked on the Moon, brought back tons of rocks, incredible pictures, adventures—proof that man could operate machinery on the Moon—and a host of other important steps that would have given mankind a leg up on space exploration.

But aside from the goal of reaching the Moon, the next step in operations was confused. Was a Moon base a jumping-off place for space exploration, or was an orbiting space station, the Soviet Union concept, a better idea? Should a base be established on the Moon, or was that rock too inhospitable for permanent colonization? Was an expedition to Mars a better goal?

"There were too many questions in the scientific community," the Guide said, "and too little money in the government coffers. Space and war couldn't coexist, and the Moon became a place that was discovered but unexplored."

I remembered a line from the movie *Apollo 13*—the failed mission to the Moon: "It's as if," I said to the Guide, "Christopher Columbus discovered the New World and decided never to return."

"In fact," the Guide said, "Christopher Columbus was predated by five hundred years by the Viking explorer Leif Eriksson. He discovered America around the year 1000—and no one decided to follow his route to the New World. It's a pretty close analogy to what happened with the Moon."

The Guide pointed at a few nearby rocks. "These asteroids are only fifty to one hundred feet in diameter, and weigh a couple of tons,'' he said. ''They are too small to be seen by the telescopes on the Moon, and are really too small to be worth hauling back for mining operations. And they are of little danger to the Earth.''

If one of these stones hit the atmosphere of Earth, it would give off a great light show as the friction of the ionosphere caused it to disintegrate. Perhaps a few chunks of it would reach the Earth and become meteorites, fist-sized chunks of heat-scarred rock that would be of vast interest to scientists and valuable to collectors. I was so close to some of these rocks I felt I could reach out and touch them.

''It's hard to realize that they are traveling at seventeen thousand miles an hour,'' the Guide said to my mind. ''Yes, it is,'' I said in reply, surprised that I could hear my own voice in the vacuum of space. I remembered then, of course, that I wasn't really in space. If I wanted to, I could see my room, I thought, but I was transfixed by this journey to the planets. The Guide stretched out his arm and pointed ahead and below where we hovered.

I saw a glint as light reflected from some object. I peered at the area and was stunned to see what looked like a shantytown in space. Boxcar-sized crates were attached by tubes that looked like refugees from a dismantled McDonald's playhouse. These tubes and crates were connected by enclosed catwalks that led to a series of geodesic domes. There was no symmetry to the structure; it wandered all over the place as if some giant child had been given the Universe's largest Erector set and had gone berserk with it.

''What is it?'' I asked the Guide.

''That's her ship,'' he said.

''That's a spaceship? Aren't spaceships sleek and saucer-shaped or look at least like a cylindrical missile? This is a bunch of junk. It's lean-to heaven. I've seen better looking habitats in the South Bronx—after they were knocked down. How in the world can that thing fly?''

''Actually,'' he said, ''it flies pretty well once you consider that it doesn't fly at all, but is pushed.''

In fact, the Guide explained, the spacecraft doesn't have

to be sleek or aerodynamically designed. There is no air in space to slow it down, so all you do is point the exhaust in the opposite direction from where you want to go, fire up the nuclear fission generator, and off you go, continually gaining speed until the generator is turned off or you run out of fuel.

"Space really isn't empty," the Guide said. "There are atoms and molecules all over the place; just not in great enough concentrations to slow down an asteroid, a planet, or even a spacecraft with any kind of propellant." He pointed to scuppers above the craft's reactor, located about a quarter mile from the snake of shacks, and attached to the conglomeration by a thin steel shaft.

"In theory, if something went wrong with the reactor, the ship could cast off the reactor and try to escape nuclear radiation damage. Radiation, not an explosion, is the main concern," he said. "First, the likelihood of an explosion is remote even in a fission reactor because of zillions of safeguards—remember even at Chernobyl there was no nuclear explosion; second, if the unthinkable occurred and the reactor did detonate, the shacks would be vaporized if they were fifty miles away.

"Third, it didn't make much difference either way because the reactor supplied all the life-support systems for the spaceship. If the reactor went bad and had to be scuttled, the crew would likely freeze to death within hours, their only escape being a couple of short-range hybrid spacecraft used for herding Earth-bound meteors loaded with usable ores toward the Moon or Mars mining operations."

Also in the ramshackle group of boxcars were a couple of air-breathing jets which could operate in an atmosphere. Nabyla has used her family fortune and the extensive engineering and mechanical abilities of both herself and her crew to get those machines assembled in space. Long before the discovery of humanoids in another star system, Nabyla had thought about the possibility of needing something that could land in an atmosphere, if only for a clandestine return to Earth. Not that it was likely even a small craft would escape someone's defenses. It had cost Nabyla a fortune to get those jets to the ship, but, fortunately, no one paid a whole lot of attention to what space cowboys did, just as long as they kept herding those asteroids away from Earth.

My thoughts returned to the structure of the spaceship itself. The Guide pointed out the features. In the front, or at least in the direction toward Jupiter and Saturn, was a dome about the size of a large two-car garage, about one thousand square feet of living space. That was the ship's operations and communications center. The dome behind that, about twice the size, was the crew's quarters. The crew of twelve men and women each had a lot of space, even though only four to six people were on duty for any stretch of time. The kitchen and dining hall were housed in a boxcar off the crew's quarters.

A boxcar behind the living quarters held the life-suspension baths where the off-duty crew slept in suspended animation for as long as a year at a time.

Behind that were the storage containers, which were always nearly empty, and then a series of boxcar-shacks that held together the combination garbage/waste/reconstitution facilities, the key to long-term space survival.

Other attachments were basically empty. One had been turned into a handball court, although the game lost a lot of meaning in zero-gravity conditions; another was converted into a garden, although plants grew strangely in outer space; another was outfitted into a brig with padded walls. Twenty years in space could sometimes make people go a little bit akilter.

We materialized between the walls of one of the boxcars. The crew was dressed very informally, in what looked like jockey shorts and T-shirts of a nondescript color. The most impressive part of the workclothes were huge boots.

"The boots are actually magnetized," the Guide explained. Without them everyone would float around in the cubicles in weightless space. The lessons learned in the space station activities in the early twenty-first century found that constant weightlessness confused the body and resulted in bone and muscle loss. By strapping on the magnets, space residents were able to get a grip on life as they once knew it and were able to maintain better muscle control.

Suddenly an orange object came hurtling directly at us. My eyes told me it was a cat, its claws extended toward us, its face contorted, its ears plastered to the side of its head. I ducked reflexively and the creature passed by us and hit the wall of the ship. It ricocheted around the spaceship, bouncing and tumbling in an effort to regain control of its gravity-free slide through space.

A woman jumped from her chair and captured the flying creature as if she were intercepting a football. She used a hand to brace herself as she neared the roof of the ship, and began stroking the nervous feline as the magnets in her boots softly dragged her toward the floor.

"What's the matter, Furball? Been seeing ghosts again?" she cooed. A couple of her crewmates chuckled.

The Guide and I exchanged glances, and we removed ourselves from the presence of the cat before we caused it to go bouncing off the walls again. "The cat could see us," I said. "Yes," the Guide said, "cats are very intuitive and exceptionally psychic."

I pondered his comments and then another obvious problem arose. "What in the world is a cat doing in space, anyway?" I asked.

"To keep the mouse population in check."

Mice in space? I knew that had to be a dream. Then suddenly a really horrible thought entered my mind: If there were mice in space, obviously because someone's experiment escaped or somehow a mouse stowed away inside a capsule, that meant there were probably cockroaches there, too. I shuddered.

"Excellent food source," the Guide said. "If you can catch them."

7

TELL ME, LORD, WHY THESE SCENES HURT MY MIND

THE SHRILL SQUEAK OF THE PORTABLE PHONE GOT MY AT-tention. I vaguely remember thinking, *I wonder how long it has been ringing.* It trilled again. I had turned the an-swering machine off because I didn't want to talk to any-one. I didn't want to go outside. I didn't want to do anything but curl up in a ball. Another trill.

"Go away. Go away. Leave me alone," I hissed at the phone. Another trill. "Why don't you get the idea that I don't want to talk to you?"

Trill. Trill.

If I get up to answer it, whoever it is will hang up just as I pick up the receiver, so why should I even bother? I thought as I struggled out of bed and plodded to the phone.

Trill. Trill.

Tr . . . "Hello," I said, in the grumpiest tone I could muster.

"Shawn, it's Ed."

"Hi." The lack of enthusiasm in my voice was palpable.

"Er, is this a bad time, Shawn? I've been trying to reach

you for days. But your answering machine hasn't been on. What's up?''

"Nothing. Nothing. I've just been feeling a little down. I don't want to do anything.''

Ed was quiet for a couple of moments. "Well, why don't you go out for a walk. That's always refreshing.''

"I don't want to go outside. No, that's not right. I can't go outside. I'm afraid to go outside.''

I've always had a bit of anxiety as well as a few other phobias. I hate to fly in airplanes. I dislike traveling any distance from New York City. I have a problem with mornings—I never get up before two in the afternoon. Most people who know me, know this.

"I see," Ed said. "How long has it been since you've been out?''

"Maybe a week; no, it's been about ten days.''

"Run out of food yet? Cigarettes?''

With a start, I scanned the table where the carton of Marlboros was and mentally pictured what was inside the box. I had only one pack.

"I'm not starving," I told him, "but I guess I need more cigarettes.''

"Soooo," he said, "what you're telling me is that you are so depressed and fearful that you are going to quit smoking rather than leave your apartment? And I thought depression was bad for people.''

I managed a chuckle. "I'm not that depressed . . . at least, I don't think I'm that depressed.'' I felt better. Whatever psychological magic Ed knew was working, showing me once again that he had some psychic powers and knew how to use them even if he wouldn't admit it.

"In fact, I'm taking out a cigarette now.'' I paused to light it, flicking my Bic next to the speaker on the telephone. I knew that would upset him. I have this depraved desire to torment my friends who are former smokers.

"You don't have to do this on my account," he said.

I inhaled noisily, then exhaled with audible satisfaction.

"Well, it's your dime," I said.

"I was just concerned that I hadn't heard from you in a while, and every time I called no one picked up. It's also unlike you not to have the answering machine on. And now, I realize, you've been having some problems."

I crushed the cigarette in the ashtray. It no longer satisfied me. "I'm not sure, Ed. Whenever I go outside, a thousand sensations accost me at once. A truck coughs, and I see bombs exploding; a car squeals, and I hear thousands of voices in anguish; the WALK sign blinks, and my head throbs with indecision. And that's before I've taken a dozen steps. I can't even get to the corner before I run back into the house. I'm so terrified that I don't even lock the door because I'm afraid my hands will shake so much I won't be able to use the key to open the door."

"It's not the first time this has happened to you, Shawn. Why do you think it's happening now? Do you think it has to do with the visions, with the Guide?"

"I know that's what it is. I'm really worried. My friend's mother, when she found out what I was doing with the Guide, launched into a tirade, accusing me of unnatural, ungodly, blasphemous deeds. I tried to laugh it off, but I guess it really got me."

I lit another cigarette.

"Shawn, are you telling me that you are unsure about what your visions are showing you? Are you concerned about the veracity of what you see?"

"No, I'm sure I see what I see, but I'm unsure if I should tell anyone about it. If I'm right, will I rob the future of hope? If I'm wrong will I create turmoil and upset people for no reason? It's all the old arguments that psychics face from the time they are children: The world doesn't really want to know what is going to happen, especially if it is bad news. If something good happens, it's a coincidence; if something bad occurs, it's the psychic's fault."

I sucked on the Marlboro, watching the red tip devour the tobacco, and pulled a long tug of nicotine and tars into my lungs. *God, does that feel good*, I said to myself.

"We've had this discussion before, Shawn. You are really concerned about the nature of your prophecies," Ed said.

He went on, "You know, just the other evening I was talking with one of my friends, Bruce Sylvester, a minister and theologian here in Florida, and we were talking about the problems of being a psychic or a prophet. 'Prophets don't foretell the future, Ed. They are forthtelling. It's what the future looks like from the point of view we have today. It is what is coming forth and what is coming forth can be changed if people change in reaction to what is being said. Don't be afraid to be a forthteller.' ''

I took another drag on the cigarette and then punched it into oblivion. ''That's almost exactly what the Guide said, isn't it?''

''Just what I was thinking.''

''So maybe I'm not an agent of Satan after all.'' We both laughed.

''Maybe not. But something you said interested me, Shawn. When you went outside, you said the WALK sign made your head throb. Sit down and relax a minute . . .''

I was sitting. I put my fingers to my temples and began rubbing them lightly, in a circular motion—an exercise that helps calm me down and reduces tension.

''. . . and tell me what is causing all the indecision. What's making your head throb? What is it that you feel? What do you see . . . ?''

8

THE GUESTS BEGIN THE JOURNEY TO EARTH

THE MALE RAISED HIS HEAD FROM HIS CHEST, AND HIS LIDS twitched. Then his head dropped back to his chest.

"The he-bug is waking up, Nabyla," Davis said, jabbing his leader with a finger in the ribs.

Nabyla turned away from Davis so he couldn't see her roll her eyes. *He-bug? The goon has already come up with a slur for these people. Did I really call him a person? Are they people? If they weren't born on Earth or if they aren't children of Earthlings can they be humans?*

A chill ran through her spine. She muttered, "What if they are children of humans? What if they and we . . . No, it can't be. It's just coincidental. God, I'd love to take a look at their DNA."

The spaceship homes of the asteroid cowboys had a ton of technical equipment, including major medical-repair paraphernalia that was computer driven. There was also a virtual surgery linkup. After all, when the nearest doctor is a hundred million miles away you'd better have a lot of supplies handy.

But no one had thought there would be any need to do DNA analysis while hunting asteroids between Jupiter and Mars. So the DNA sequencers and analyzers that any kid could buy at Sears for a third-grade science project weren't on board the ship.

As Nabyla measured out another dose for a tranquilizing dart, she mentally calculated the next steps for her project to succeed. It was 2108, and it was going to take at least eighteen years to get back home. After being missing for thirty-six years, she and her crew would suddenly pop up on someone's radar screen like a lost flight from the Bermuda Triangle, and then get their just rewards.

She loaded the gun, unbuckled herself from the seat, and floated around to where the male was stirring, not that he was going to be able to do much moving with his arms and legs bound together with tape. His head popped up again and his eyes opened. The glaze began to disperse and knowledge rushed at him at the speed of light. Before he could comprehend the figure floating before him, Nabyla fired the tranquilizer gun, and the dart stung into his shoulder. The male made an odd screech, spotted the dart, and made an attempt to snatch it out of his skin with his teeth. But the drug was already relaxing his muscle reflexes. In another instant he was unconscious again. Nabyla checked the other two aliens. They, too, were out of it. She checked the pulse of the male child and felt a strong response.

The home ship was in sight, and Davis expertly maneuvered the hybrid's thrusters to line up with the craft's hold. The craft glided into place without a hitch. "Hah," said Davis, "it's as easy as parallel parking on First Avenue."

Nabyla shrugged. She assumed Davis was talking about finding a parking space in New York City, but that wasn't a problem. Rotating wheels had been standard on cars since 2006. She remembered that some of the antique cars only had maneuverable front wheels and realized that was Davis's reference. Davis kept talking about the collection of cars from the twentieth century he had at his parents' home on Earth. By the time he returned he would have been presumed dead for thirty-six years and would have been away for forty years.

Those cars are rust and dust now, Davis, she said to herself. Those automobiles were his pride and joy. He'd be devastated if he realized they were gone. She felt a glimmer of sympathy for Davis, until she spotted him leering at the bare-breasted alien female.

"For bugs, they're not all that tough to look at, either."

"Keep looking at her that way, Davis, and I'll mention your comments to Luba."

Davis reddened. His spacemate was fiercely possessive, and Davis—although twice her size—was truly terrified of her. He understood that the threats she made regarding disembowelment were not idle banter. And if he didn't understand it, certainly every woman on board did.

Davis returned to his duties of locking down the aircraft and remotely closing the hold's outer doors. Once the outer doors were closed, the hold would be pressurized, and the hybrid crew and its precious cargo would be greeted by Redmond, Luba, Warrick, and Samantha. The rest of the crew was in the baths. Nabyla could hardly wait for her turn in the baths. She could really use the rest.

The baths had never bothered Nabyla. The courses at the Academy in Tupper Lake had trained her to understand the concept of oxygenated fluids and to fight to overcome her instincts: That breathing water could be good for you— especially if you wanted to wake up rested, sharp, and not a day older after a year-long nap. The oxygenated fluid system also made space travel easier on the explorer and more practical.

Interestingly, the idea behind oxygenated fluids was an offshoot of attempts at suspended animation. In the late 1970s and early 1980s, some fringe scientists started freezing the recently deceased in vats of liquid nitrogen in hopes of keeping them incorrupt until such time as a cure for the disease that killed them was discovered.

Then the frozen body could be thawed and cured. Early experiments proved you could freeze some amphibians and then defrost them without consequence. The experimenters even managed the procedure with a dog, who didn't forget any tricks when its body temperature was brought back to normal.

Researchers were stymied by the problem of reviving a person who was dead before being frozen. Since there were few takers among those who were still alive to be flash frozen without a reasonable guarantee of an uneventful defrost, the movement was ground to a halt. Things got a lot worse for theory when one of the pioneers of the movement was charged with beheading a patient, possibly before the patient was legally dead, in order to freeze the head to permit later revival when a few problems had been resolved—chief of which was how to reconnect the head to a viable body.

Concurrently with these rogue experiments, doctors were trying to develop substances which could help premature babies survive common lung disorders created when the child was born before the lung tissue was mature enough to allow breathing on its own. Many of these babies died from the lung disease or were permanently blinded by overuse and improper use of oxygen.

The use of oxygen tended to create the development of unnecessary and fragile blood vessels in the eye, and when these blood vessels ruptured the resultant scarring tended to cause the retina to detach in the eye. Surgical repair of the detached retina did not have a good success rate.

So the idea arose, first tested in 2009, when the world's first surviving octuplets were born in Baltimore, of reimmersing newborns into an oxygenated fluid that closely duplicated conditions in the placenta. The tiny babies, none of them weighing more than a pound at birth, stayed in the fluid baths for as long as three months before being taken from the liquid and delivered into an air-breathing world.

The use of the baths created its own vital statistic controversy by those who claimed the child's birth date was the day it was removed from the mother; others claimed that one could not be born until one was an air breather and weaned from the pseudo-placentas. The debate raged on for decades until it became common practice to remove all babies from the womb prior to birth. The official birth date became the day the child was removed from the bath incubators.

As scientists perfected the oxygenated liquid baths, other

researchers came up with the idea of using the baths as suspended-animation chambers. Once a person's lungs adapted to the oxygenated fluids, the temperature of the baths was slowly dropped until the person's body temperature was fifteen degrees cooler. At that temperature, cellular activity slowed, sometimes slowing too much and causing the heart to stop. A pacemaker on a wire was swallowed. The monitor triggered an effective electric shock to keep the heart beating in these cases.

Experiments on head injury cases in the 2030s proved that the system worked and could maintain a person in suspended animation for six months or longer. The use of the system for space travel and long-term space duties was immediately considered as one of the future uses of the baths. When the meteor disaster emergency occurred, and it became obvious that people were going to have to spend years in space to monitor the chunks of rock, the suspended animation baths went along with the asteroid cowboys into space. The bath were used extensively on the IBM-Exxon mission to Alpha Centauri, with crew members spending as long as two years at a stretch in the baths without any ill effects. By the time Nabyla was going through the Academy, everyone had to undergo suspended animation and know how to run the computerized baths, including troubleshooting and emergency-resuscitation techniques.

I don't think Redmond has ever forgiven me for the baths, Nabyla thought to herself with a chuckle. When she and Redmond met at the fateful restaurant in Greater Albany, they had never really discussed future plans. Nabyla knew she wanted to be a space cowboy at least to keep her parents' and grandparents' accomplishments from dictating her life. Redmond just wanted to be with Nabyla, so he joined the space corps as well. His Harvard education served him well in the courses, especially the studies involving the intricacies of astronomy and the mathematics of space travel.

But Redmond's real skill came in his ability to organize. He created schedules for everything. They weren't hardened, compartmentalized, written-in-stone orders, but he was confident enough with them to know when certain things had to be done and what others could slide. He was the perfect cook, knowing exactly when to start making the bread so that it would be ready to pop in the oven as soon as he took the turkey out of the stove. The bread would be hot as soon as the vegetables finished steaming, the soup was simmering, and he'd completed a surgical dissection of the bird.

So planned were his holiday feasts that not only was the meal for at least a dozen people served on time—he was able to join the rest of the guests at the dinner table.

Redmond decided to spend the rest of his life with Nabyla because he was in love with her and because he had nowhere else to go. His family, for whom he was named, made it plain that he was unwelcome at home, where his parents were raising a second family. His sisters had married and, because they looked so much like each other, they vowed never to be in the same room together.

Nabyla was his life raft. He'd known too many other Cloningers who had gone to Kevorkian camps even though they were in perfect health. One friend had told him, "Living with the dying has made me more alive than before. I love working here. And eventually I'll die here, too."

Redmond's decision to pursue space-based home economics stunned those who saw him as captain material. "No," said Redmond to his Academy adviser, "space is going to be my home and I'm going to make it the best home possible." When he and Nabyla were assigned to the *Harley*, he found no objections to his role as chief cook and bottle washer. He handled the roles of chef, janitor, and scheduler with finesse. His times in the baths were a problem for the crew because they were accustomed to Redmond's keeping things in order and preparing edible foods under trying circumstances.

The rest of the crew hated to see Redmond climb into the baths; but no one hated it as much as Redmond. He could never simply open his mouth and let the oxygenated fluid pour down his throat and into his lungs. He would hold his breath—once as long as four minutes, thirty-five seconds, according to the crew pool on the subject—before gasping in the fluid. Then he would thrash around for several seconds before realizing that his lungs were processing the oxygen in the fluid and he was not drowning.

Then Redmond would refuse to relax and accept the cooling temperatures of suspended animation. He would fight to stay awake, before succumbing to the chill and slipping into semiconsciousness. He was the only crew member who noticeably aged during the trip, persuading Nabyla and the others that it was imperative for him to miss one or two or three turns in the baths.

The effects of the baths was to turn an eighteen-year mission to a distant star into a two-to-three-year mission as far as the person's physical aging was concerned. More importantly, early experimentation showed that audible information, such as news broadcasts, were heard, understood, and remembered by people in the baths while under suspended animation. That meant they could be kept up-to-date on progress made by the ship as it flew through space as well as what was going on at home. People could sleep for two years and not wake up with two-year gaps in their knowledge.

The development of the baths made travel to the stars practical and possible. In Nabyla's crew, only four to six people were awake at any one time. But there were only eight baths and now they had fifteen people to deal with. *Some people are going to age physically as well as chronologically*, she thought. *We are going to need a very big reward for this*.

When the cargo hold pressurized, Davis and Nabyla popped the latches on the hybrid. Nabyla began taking the duct tape off the aliens, all three of whom were still unconscious and showing no signs of coming to.

Warrick walked up to the ship with the recording log, and Nabyla approached him. "On our exploratory trip to the surface, we encountered a group of humanoids who indicated through signs their desire to board our ship and visit our home planet," she lied. "They indicated a preference to be rendered unconscious during the trip to the spacecraft and were administered tranquilizers by injection. There were no incidents on board and the aliens arrived on board the *Harley* in excellent health.

"Since they will be unaccustomed to our ship, we will place them in the safe room until they have learned to deal with zero gravity and better communications can be arranged. We will videotape their activity in an attempt to learn more about them. We will also administer AEs to the group." She signed off with her name and rank, time and date, and recorded the persons present.

She had almost forgotten about the AEs. While baths made long-term space flight practical, AEs—antiemetics—made it livable.

Since the first trips into space, one of the less publicized problems had been the predisposition of the toughest space pioneers to suffer nausea and vomiting in space. Not only is constant retching a pain to the person suffering emesis, it isn't terribly pleasant for others in the crew who have to dodge globules of vomitus. And worse, of course, was the fact that one person's losing his or her stomach made the rest of the crew nauseous—as people who fly in large passenger airplanes find out when the plane hits turbulence.

Mankind has been using natural and synthetic antiemetics for centuries. Ginger is considered to have antiemetic properties and children have been given ginger ale for generations when they suffer vomiting attacks. Chemical antiemetics were developed for helping people combat the emesis that occurs with the administration of cancer chemotherapy. Most of those compounds rarely helped as stronger and stronger anticancer drugs—especially cisplatinum and its cousins—were developed during the 1970s and 1980s.

Effective emesis control didn't come about until the 1990s with the development of chemicals that blocked vomiting signals from the stomach from reaching the brain, and also stopped signals from the brain reaching the stomach. About the time these drugs became well accepted, scientists began changing the nature of chemotherapy to relying on gene therapy and targeted cells The heavy duty chemotherapy drugs fell out of favor and the need for the antiemetics also dropped.

But fortunately those drugs were available on the shelf when the boom in space exploration began in the twenty-first century. AEs were taken along with every morning meal by every crew member in space. The oral form was usually administered, but the aliens would be given injections. No one wanted to put their hands near the aliens' teeth. No one knew how they would react.

Nabyla would assume that no one would believe a word of her report, but that problem would have to work itself out. Warrick, in addition to being in charge of the ship's supplies and crediting reports and bath schedules, was the *Harley*'s psychologist, a required crew member on the long contract spacecraft. The *Harley* and ships like her, in the hands of someone who went space crazy, could do an immense amount of damage to ecosystems. A nuclear core, for example, dropped on a space dome somewhere could wipe out a colony. Earth-based contractors who hired the crews and reaped profits from their activities wanted to make sure someone was in charge who could deal with the most prevalent problem in space—cabin fever.

Someone who could deal with relationship dynamics was needed, too. Spacemates—married couples, associated living pairs, etc., depending on the formalization of their arrangement—went on the job together, and there was always a chance that conflicts would develop. The pairs were always on duty together and were put in baths together. Warrick's job was to make sure relationships stayed on an even keel. Jealousy and adultery and cheating in space could prove deadly to a lot of people.

Warrick's partner, Samantha, was the one member of the crew who did virtually nothing—and every one was happy about it. She was the *Harley* nuclear engineer. If anything went wrong with the power system, the lifeline for the ship, Sam had to handle it.

Fortunately for her and the *Harley*, the nuclear drives worked so well and so effortlessly that her only job was to inspect the drive before she took her bath. Her bath was tied to the computer drive so if there was so much as a blip on the drive, her bath was immediately heated. A computer voice began a verbal output of the crisis even as the thawing process was taking place. In the twenty-one years that the *Harley* had been operating—both in its role as an asteroid spotter and as a rogue vessel—Sam had never had an unscheduled awakening. It took about eight hours for a complete awakening to occur; most experts believed that if the drive developed a critical problem, it would have to be corrected within four hours.

Sam, when she was awake, tended to read a lot, and during their awake sessions en route to Alpha Centauri, she and Warrick had spent hours trying to devise methods of communicating with the aliens.

"So," said Warrick, "when do you think we should let Earth know we are alive? If we signal now, they won't hear about it for four years anyway."

"I think," Nabyla said, "that we had better keep this information to ourselves until we are back in the Sol system. These people have to survive weightlessness; they have to survive the baths, and they have to survive our food for eighteen years. I don't want to announce anything prematurely and then bring in some corpses."

Davis chimed in, "If we are a surprise to Earth, it gives us the advantage in negotiations. Remember, we've got a lot to explain. Disappearing with a billion dollars in equipment isn't going to make anyone happy."

Heads bobbed in agreement. Warrick said he would prepare an announcement for the rest of the crew still in their baths and make sure there was concurrence among them once they were awakened. Nabyla could have simply decided the course of action by fiat, but she had long ago decided that people who faced mining tungsten from a Jovian moon for the rest of their lives should be able to vote on decisions that could result in imprisonment.

Warrick and Samantha volunteered to spend an additional six months awake in order to monitor, feed, and acclimate the aliens to life aboard the *Harley*. Warrick had dabbled in the sometimes bizarre psychiatric field of creative linguitism. He'd enchant fellow *Harley* crew members with tales of how some children in remote settings often developed their own languages. Now he'd have the opportunity to try and figure out the language—if indeed, the aliens had a language—of their "guests."

9

THE ALIENS AWAKE TO A FLOATING SENSATION

RANAN STIRRED FIRST, HER LEFT HAND SQUEEZING THE fabric of the cell. She kneaded it for a few seconds, then quickly opened her eyes. She reflexively rubbed her thigh where the dart had hit her.

The light in the room was deliberately set low. Ranan swiveled her head in search of the light and then let out a sharp cry as she realized she was floating in the air, about twelve inches from the nominal floor of the cell. Tethers with Velcro straps around her ankles kept her from floating away.

Her brain began processing a vast amount of new knowledge. She found her son nearby, also tethered to the floor. He was still unconscious. Asorg, her mate, was lying on the surface of the cell, his breathing causing him to rise and fall with each inhale and exhale while the tethers held him in place.

Ranan noted with satisfaction that they all seemed to be uninjured, but her brain could not comprehend why they were floating.

She examined the tethers and began working the straps. The crew had not wanted to imprison the aliens in the cell, but they didn't want them floating around the room until the aliens could figure out what could be done in weightlessness and what could not be achieved.

She was able to open the strap on her left ankle first. And having discovered the secret of Velcro, she quickly freed herself from the tethers, pushing off the floor with her left foot in triumph. Immediately she began to tumble toward the nominal ceiling of the cell. She screamed Asorg's name, but the unconscious male failed to respond. Ranan thudded into the ceiling, back first, and slowly ricocheted toward a wall, her arms flailing helplessly as she caromed off the wall and toward the floor again. She attempted to control herself by spreading her arms and flapping them like a bird, but she wasn't able to control her legs, which flipped over her head as the tumble roll continued. In desperation she reached out one arm and snagged the tether holding the child. She hit the floor and bounced again, but was able to maintain a hold as the child's tethers halted her movement.

The child opened its eyes and smiled at his mother, calling, ''Ranan.'' The child tried to rub its neck, still sore from where he was struck by Nabyla's dart, and found his arms firmly held by the tethers. Panic crossed his face as he tried to muscle his way out of the straps.

Ranan spoke to him in a series of sounds and grunts, which were dutifully recorded on audio and videotape. Warrick, who was watching in real time, quickly patched the sounds into a voice-recognition computer and configured the system to attempt to develop a language base for the aliens. *Ranan,* he said to himself. *Is that her name or does it mean mother?* He typed the query into the computer. He realized that the woman and the child were conversing. They had a language. It might be possible to learn to converse with these creatures.

The world suddenly brightened for Warrick. With even the crudest tools, it shouldn't take long for the aliens and the Earthmen to develop suitable ways of conversing with each other. Perhaps even an alien dictionary could be developed before they reached Earth. *We've got eighteen years to figure them out,* he thought.

The female slowly removed one of the child's tethers, speaking to him constantly. The child's eyes were wide. Ranan unhooked the Velcro and held the child motionless as he got to his feet. Then she let go. The child froze in position, then began to float, drifting away from Ranan. In her haste to grab him, she bounced one foot on the floor and started somersaulting away from the child. He screamed, "Ranan," but the forcefulness of his exhale pushed him farther away. When he turned to see where he was headed, he began an uncontrolled tumble. Ranan flattened out her trajectory and timed her path so her feet touched the padded far wall first. With almost perfect timing she recoiled across the cell toward the child, but she missed him by a foot. This time she wasn't ready for the impact with the side of the cell and tumbled toward the floor. Meanwhile, the boy was panicking, propelling himself faster and faster off the walls as he made contact with them. Eventually, the two bodies collided, and the female grabbed the child. She held him tightly, and neither moved. As they settled toward the floor, Ranan reached out and grabbed one of the loose tethers. She fastened it to the child's arm, then used his body to guide her in place to another tether and Velcroed herself in place.

She was close enough to the older male to touch him with an outstretched leg. "Asorg," she said. "Asorg." She gently nudged him.

Warrick, who was having laughing fits while watching the mother and child bounce off the walls, quickly wrote: "Asorg. Name or 'wake up'?" He spoke the same information into the microphone of the voice-recognition computer.

The male stirred. He was conscious almost instantly and, remembering how the last time he opened his eyes he had been shot with a dart gun, he tried to protect himself with his hands. That led him to discover he was shackled. He let out a grunt of agony, and with catlike urgency looked over his surroundings.

His face changed from anger and terror when he saw the

female and the child. He thrashed angrily at the bindings, attempting to pull them apart with brute strength. "Asorg," the female said. She used another expression, and the male stopped thrashing. She seemed to be trying to relate her experiences, using a free hand to indicate flying. The male scrutinized her as if she had lost her mind. She talked to the child, calling to him as "Sorgan," and the child swung his body around and clasped his legs around her waist. She then slowly and deliberately undid the Velcro.

The male understood, raised his arm to his mouth and, using his teeth, separated the Velcro. With his free arm he snatched the other Velcro tether, then dived to free his feet. The female and child both were yelling "nigroth," but the male tore off the last Velcro snap and immediately began a series of midair cartwheels that resulted in a jarring, feet-first impact with the ceiling, and a series of bounces off walls until he was close enough to the female to be grabbed and retethered.

He sat panting, one leg held firmly, the other rising by itself. The aliens sat hunched together and began talking rapidly. Warrick seemed to detect an argument between the male and female. She seemed to be comforting him; he seemed to be annoyed by the comfort.

Suddenly, the male spread his hands wide and the three grasped hands and formed a three-way circle. They all began some kind of chant, and then raised their heads toward the ceiling and were quiet. The male intoned a few words. The trio squeezed their hands together and bobbed silently in the weightlessness. They bowed their heads for several moments, then, as if a firecracker had gone off, suddenly stared at a spot near the ceiling and began speaking.

Warrick felt the hair on the back of his neck tingle, and cold sweat escaped the pores under his arms and ran down his sides. *What in the world are they looking at?* he wondered. He studied the speech patterns of the aliens. They weren't talking to each other, but seemed to be addressing the area above where their eyes appeared to focus. Warrick found himself changing the camera angle to try and get a view of what the group was seeing, but all that was discernible was the padded ceiling. He turned his attention to the aliens and gasped as all three of them were staring directly at the point where the observation camera was focused.

Warrick rubbed the dry corners of his mouth and worked out the complexities of what he was seeing: These were people with no apparent knowledge of electricity or technology; they didn't even have knowledge of the wheel; they couldn't have knowledge of television, cameras, or anything like video transmission; they should not have been able to see the camera—even though Warrick knew the camera's location, when he was in the room he couldn't spot it.

The aliens stood up and each pointed with one hand directly to the location of a camera.

Warrick was transfixed. The aliens were waving at him.

10

THE PSYCHIC WORLD IS A FOG THAT BRINGS MESSAGES

WHEN WINTER COMES TO NEW YORK, IT SOMETIMES snows, it sometimes sleets, it sometimes rains with wind that cuts through your body like a cold laser and chills you to the bone. None of that bothers me, or at least doesn't bother me as much as those days when the sky is overcast and the fog never quite lifts off the ground.

That's when my friends are likely to hear my voice—over the telephone. I can use the Internet, but I need the voice of someone who isn't facing the same scenery as I am to pull me out of my weather-related funks.

"Shawn, it's good to hear from you again," Ed said. "I was just thinking of you because I was working on a new project, writing a story about dowsing."

The ancient art of the dowser. A person could take a Y-shaped branch—I was always partial to hickory—grasp one end of the V in each hand so the long single end pointed straight ahead, then walk around until the long end suddenly exerted enough pressure to rotate downward. Where the stick pointed down was water.

Some dowsers claim they can use the stick to find gold or silver in rock fields; others say they can dowse oil by holding the stick over a map a thousand miles away from the site. I always stick to water. That's where I've been successful.

"Dowsing, huh? Did you try it?"

"Yeah. It was really surprising. All of a sudden the stick just seemed to have a life of its own and pointed straight down," Ed said, a catch of awe in his voice.

"Ed, you know you have to be psychic to be a successful dowser. I tell you you have the power. Just use it. So, what happened? Was there water there?"

"Of course," he said, a little irritation showing. "This is Florida. The land of homes without basements—because the water table is only four feet down. Of course I hit water. I'd like to try it in Arizona."

"Why don't you go to Arizona then?" I suggested.

"I need an editor that's going to pay for a trip to Arizona, Shawn. Now I can dutifully report that dowsing works, at least in Florida . . . So, as Barbra would say, 'What's up, Doc?' "

"The weather. Why else would I call?"

"Didn't realize things were that bad in the Big Apple. It's cold, I know, but I hadn't heard about any storm."

"It . . . it's foggy," I said, my voice revealing my distress.

"Oh."

He knew, as most of my friends know, that fog upsets me. That's because many of my most fateful psychic images come to me through a foglike haze. It's a haze that comes from my subconscious, not from Mother Nature, but there are times when I'm not sure if I'm having a vision or just dealing with New York weather.

"Well, Shawn, since you brought up the subject, I've wanted to talk to you about your visions, especially those that develop in fog. When did you first realize that the fogs were harbingers of the future? What did you see?"

Actually, what I first saw in my psychic visions occurred when I was just a child. I would be asleep or nearly asleep when the fog would roll in on my mind. I believe that for the longest time I just assumed that was how people went to sleep, in this foglike state.

I remember how figures would emerge from the fog, or perhaps it was the fog which was subsiding, because I still can't be sure if those figures ever moved. Some of them I recognized as old people who once lived down the street but had died; another time I thought I was seeing a cousin and later found out he had died of cancer a couple of years earlier in another state. My parents had never told me about it until I told them I'd seen him in my dream.

That freaked them I'm sure. I was still only seven or eight when I began remembering that these dreams often imparted information to me that I should have had no way of knowing. And that information was almost always correct, and usually was bad news. My parents and friends began to shun me and accuse me of conjuring events. I was confused and bewildered and frightened. If the messages I was getting in the fogs were bad things, then was I an agent of evil? Could I make things happen? Was it better to forget the fogs, and could I make them go away?

I found out that I could reject the fogs and their messages, but by the time I was in my teens I knew that I had some kind of power, and these fog dreams were important. I again began to focus on them when they occurred. Sometimes the messages were crystal clear; other times just as foggy as the weather. But fog always bothered me.

"If you had never tried to make the fog dreams vanish, how effective do you think you would be as a psychic?" Ed asked.

"I think it would have enhanced my ability ten times. But what happened to me occurs to a lot of psychics. They are told at a young age that what they are capable of doing is not right, and they are encouraged to ignore their abilities. Children like to please their elders, so many psychics go through a denial period. If you don't use the power, you lose it."

"You say that in those dreams you see people you once knew who have died?"

"Often, yes."

"Do you think that these apparitions appear to you because they want to or because you ask to talk to them?''

''I don't really know. I've never thought about it, but it seems that maybe I want to see them.''

''Shawn, to whom do you think the aliens were talking?''

11

So how would you teach an alien to use the toilet?

"Do we really have to do this?" Sam moaned.

"It's going to be easier to do this now than have to clean up the mess later. Besides we have to show them how much alike we are," Warrick said. He checked the weapons, putting the sonic control on stun. He had half a dozen charges, and he and Sam were wearing the magnetic boots so they would be stable if the aliens decided to attack.

Warrick approached the aliens with trepidation. He recognized that they were intelligent; they were learning quickly how to maneuver in zero gravity, showing off their muscularity. All of them, including the child, looked powerful enough to do serious damage if they had an inclination to attack. Warrick didn't mention it to Sam, but he believed the aliens possessed other knowledge and abilities that went beyond the normal senses. They had to rely on sight, sound, smell, and touch far more than Warrick and the crew, whose personal senses had been dulled by centuries of tech-

75

nology. Warrick also wondered about whether the aliens had other senses as well.

He checked the remote viewer on his wrist and determined that the aliens were on the far side of the room. He placed his palm on the door plate and half the wall of the cell raced sideways and disappeared. Warrick and Sam moved inside. "Close," he said, and the wall reappeared. The aliens hurled themselves backward and would have caromed off the walls, but they had tethered themselves loosely. The eyes traced the forms of Sam and Warrick and then stopped as they recognized the weapons in the Earthmen's hands.

"You first," he said to Sam, who gave him a withering look.

"Ranan!" she called. The female's head snapped toward Sam. Sam motioned her to come to her. The female stood rooted. Sam shrugged and walked over to the wall close to the doorway. She located a lever and pulled it. A white porcelain bowl appeared as the closet wall vanished. "Watch them, not me," Sam ordered Warrick. He smiled and kept his attention on the aliens, who were staring at Sam. Sam stepped out of her pants and panties and stepped into the cubicle and urinated. A suction fan located in the cubicle provided enough power to keep the urine particles from floating off into space.

She finished and wiped herself with tissue hanging on the roll and tossed the tissue into the void at the back of the cubicle. She pulled on her pants and made an elaborate demonstration of locating the lever and closing the cubicle door. "This is the most embarrassing thing I've ever done," Sam complained. "Now it's your turn."

Warrick called, "Asorg." The alien tried to show that he wasn't surprised at hearing his name, but this was one alien who would never be good at poker. Warrick motioned Asorg to join him at the cubicle. He remained motionless. Warrick returned to the cubicle, opened it, and removed his pants and proceeded to urinate into the cubicle. When he finished he looked back to see if there was any reaction from the group. He saw that the child was holding his genitalia and had a look of urgency about him.

"The kid has to go bad," Warrick said.

"I know. Let's leave and hopefully they will figure it out, and we won't have to hose the place down."

"Open," said Warrick, and the door disappeared. They stepped out. Warrick placed his palm on the panel and the room was secure again.

The two climbed down the corridor and into another boxcar, through a second corridor, and into the control room. Warrick sat down and checked the monitor. All three aliens were gathered around the cubicle, which they had already opened and the child was emptying his bladder. All of a sudden Sam and Warrick glanced at each other and felt instant shame.

"They are people," Warrick said, "and we are treating them like pets."

"They're aliens," Sam said, "and don't forget that they are our tickets for the future—a future on Earth in real gravity with real food and real water and real comforts. We won't have to spend our lives in space. We are going to be heroes. Don't get too close to the aliens."

A scary thought went through Sam's mind. *In eighteen years will anyone on Earth be able to tell us apart?*

With her fork, Nabyla batted the round green vegetable thing that was supposed to be a pea into the glob of fluffy white stuff that had the consistency of and tasted like mashed potatoes.

But it wasn't a pea or mashed potatoes. Nabyla knew what it was and that reduced her appetite level even farther.

Food has always been a problem in space. Until the first farms began producing crops on the Moon in 2011, nothing had successfully grown outside the Earth's atmosphere except for some particularly stubborn strains of athlete's foot and certain urinary tract infections.

The development of the Earth-to-space cannon that was used to supply the Earth-orbit space station in 2005 was a major improvement in sending supplies into space. But a forty-five-g punch into space did not allow the survivability of tomatoes, eggs, or even a radish, all of which were reduced to mush by the thrust of the cannon.

But powdered milk, eggs, potatoes, etc., made the trip
with ease. Tons of dried and powdered food were fired into
space to help feed the Moon colony and later to be ferried
out to Mars and the Jupiter moons, and from there shuttlecraft would bring tons of the material to the ministations
such as the *Harley*.

You can't eat powdered food without a moistening agent,
and there is no water in space. The only way water could
reach the Moon or the ships was to bring it up from Earth
in the Space Shuttle and then distribute it packet by packet.
It was extraordinarily expensive—the single most expensive item in space. It was, by far, too expensive to be pissed
away. Every drop of moisture that was excreted by humans
in space was captured by various mechanisms on board,
and from there was funneled to a reconstitutor, which pu-
rified the human wastes, separated water from other matter,
and recirculated it.

Once you realize what the mashed potatoes were made
from, it made them a whole lot less tasty.

Nabyla weighed fifteen pounds less since she went into
space and she had been trim to start. As she pushed the
peas around under the plate bubble which prevented them
from floating into the air around the Mess Hall, Nabyla's
mind wandered to that first message from the IBM-Exxon
crew.

Already starting its third year in space, the *Harley* crew
entertained itself by intercepting messages being sent
through space. Any decent scanner picked up the messages,
and the crew had satisfaction in knowing that they were
getting news from the Alpha Centauri probe at least fifteen
minutes before Earth-based stations could pick it up.

The signals received in 2090 that the mission had located
humanoid life on the Alpha Centauri system were reason
enough for Nabyla to order the entire crew awakened. For
several days they listened to the broadcasts and found how
close the crew had come to actually retrieving an alien before being driven off by injuries and a hostile planet.

With all twelve crew members up and alert, Nabyla recognized that perhaps this was a time for her and the crew
to do something historic. For days the group muttered about

history calling and what their role in it could be.

"OK, guys," she started the special meeting, "we've been talking about it for a week now. Do we want to stay here for another twenty years roping rocks, or do we want to be the first group to bring back a live specimen?

"Think about the fame of being the first to show off an alien life-form to the Earth. Think about the money we can earn doing that. Also think about the notoriety if we fail or if we aren't first. We might never be allowed home again."

She had their attention. "We'll make a decision in twenty-four hours. If there are any objections, we won't go. If I say go and everyone else agrees and Warrick says no, we don't do it. We've got twenty-four hours to figure out what we have to do to make this work."

Luck was smiling on them. Just two days earlier, Mack, the deliveryman, had made his yearly visit to the outpost, giving the crew full cargoes of what passed as food and even a thousand pounds of water. Supplies would not be as major a problem. But that was just the food for one year—they would be gone close to forty. Nabyla had been ordering full meal service for the crew for two years and had one full year's supply in storage, just in case Mack developed engine trouble. Because no one ate as much in space owing to mental appetite suppression, Nabyla actually had three years of food available, plus that which was in the reconstitutor. No one would even consider ingesting that gunk, no matter how palatable it could be made to look. In theory, the reconstitutor could make three years' worth of food supplies last indefinitely.

Anderson was given the task of figuring out how the crew could take off and escape without monitors on Earth and Mars figuring out that they were on their way to Alpha Centauri and had no authority to do so.

At the appropriate time, each member of the crew presented the problems and others figured out the answers. Anderson presented her plan to escape detection. No one thought it could possibly work, but when the vote was taken, the *Harley* voted 12–0 to go hunting for an alien.

"*Harley* to Mars operations. Come in, Chuck."

They waited three minutes—at virtually the speed of

light it still took radio signals ninety seconds to reach Mars from the *Harley*'s position on the far edge of the Asteroid Belt, close to the rings of Jupiter. Then there was the nominal wait until Chuck could wake up, figure out who was squawking at him, and return the call.

"*Harley*, Mars base here. How y'all doing out there? Haven't heard from you guys in a month o' Sundays." He rattled on and on about everything from the World Series to his grandchildren on the Moon.

Nabyla turned to the crew, who were listening to the exchanges. "If you were so worried about us, Chuck, why haven't you called us in six months?" Chuck took a deep breath, and Nabyla took the opportunity to interject her message.

"Mars base, this is *Harley*. Listen, Chuck, we've spotted a big one, maybe one hundred to one hundred and fifty tons in an erratic orbit. We're going to chase it down. It's headed toward the back side of Jupiter. We are heating up the nuke drive now and will pursue it. We will either track it and make sure it stays in orbit; we'll see if it smacks Jupiter; or we'll lasso it and hold it for pickup and transport. Copy?"

In the ninety seconds it took to send the messages and the four seconds before Chuck gave them an acknowledgment, the nuclear fission drive had already pushed the ramshackle space station more than a thousand miles.

"*Harley* to Mars base. We are in pursuit of the stone. We could lose contact when we slide around the corner and follow the rock behind Jupiter. We anticipate about a week of radio silence. Copy."

Anderson's plan was to get a head start on the authorities by ducking behind Jupiter and using the Jovian gravitational force to slingshot the craft farther into space. Then the *Harley* would try to remain between Jupiter and the monitoring stations as it burned the drive on high out away from the Solar System and toward Alpha Centauri. There were faster craft around than the *Harley*, but if all went well, the *Harley* would have anywhere from a week to a month head start on a pursuit craft—provided anyone really cared enough to pursue them.

After three days at full burn, the *Harley* dipped behind Jupiter and Nabyla immediately cut its transponder and focused radar in front of them. They kept the radio on to receive incoming messages, but no one planned on returning comments for the next four decades.

As all spur-of-the-moment plans tend to work out, this one was clockwork precision. In fact, it took Mars base nearly four months to figure out that the *Harley* had never emerged from behind Jupiter. It took another six months for authorities to send out a halfhearted search party and the main purpose of the search was to try and locate the renegade asteroid Nabyla had lied about to Mars base.

Thinking back on the haste in which the mission was put together and how well it worked, Nabyla remembered the words of her great-grandfather on how to hit a baseball. "Go up there and look for the ball. When you see it, hit it. Don't think about it, just hit it. You think, you hesitate, you lose."

For two years, the amount of time it took for the *Harley* to reach its maximum speed, roughly thirty-two percent of the speed of light, the entire crew was awake. It was critical for everyone to calculate every last detail of the flight before rotating in the baths. Six months into a sleep was no time to recall that there would be no place for a visitor to sleep on the long trip home. The last thing that Nabyla remembered after she had helped Redmond into the baths and before she inhaled the fluids was intercepting a message notifying the corporate space agencies that the official search for the *Harley* had been called off, and the crew was lost.

Maybe we've just lost our minds, thought Nabyla as the numbness of the baths robbed her of consciousness. *No one will know for sure for forty years.*

THE ELDERS HAVE NO
EXPERIENCE WITH THE BATHS

WARRICK HAD NEVER FELT AS REFRESHED AND AS aroused as he did getting out of the baths. His mind was instantly alert. He could see himself winning some sort of Nobel Prize for his work in deciphering the alien language and customs. He had worked steadily with the Sorgast, as the family called itself, for two years, before the other crew members had insisted that he spend at least a year in the bath.

As the cold numbness left his limbs, the computers went through the mandatory checklist of scans to make sure his body had fully recovered. He and Asorg had even begun talking together in English. Warrick spoke to Ranan and Sorgan in their language, often producing quizzical looks from the child as Warrick butchered the tongue.

He was amazed at how readily the Sorgast understood their situation and seemed to realize that they were being taken from their home with little likelihood they would ever return. Warrick was astounded at how well the Sorgast adapted to life on the *Harley* amid myriad electronic devices that they had never before seen or imagined. The other crew members had fed Warrick regular information on the progress of the Sorgast development, including the discovery that Earthmen had strange taboos regarding sex. Ranan had insisted on garments to cover her body before she and her family—they had been united in some ceremony, the *Harley* discovered—would emerge from the brig.

Now the Sorgast and the crew wore similar garments, and the only differences seemed to be the greenish tint of the Sorgast skin. Warrick remembered some of the rhetoric of the twentieth century when men would proclaim they treated people of every color—"White, red, brown, black, or green"—the same. *Well, you bigoted cretins,* he thought with a laugh, *now you are going to get your chance to prove it.* He could almost picture the scene in his mind. "I don't care if his father killed a hormash with his bare hands, no daughter of mine is going to date some lizard-skinned heathen from another planet."

Warrick checked out with the machinery and put on his clothes. His next year with the Sorgast would be the last for a while. The Sorgast were becoming so much like the crew, aside from their skin, that Nabyla was concerned they would be considered a hoax. She wanted to make sure that Sorgan, at least, was still a child when they reached Earth. He was now about eight years old. All the women on the crew could easily be tested for pregnancies while on board, so unless the crew was capable of creating a child out of thin air, the only explanation for Sorgan would be the correct one: That he was the child of Asorg and Ranan and they were from Alpha Centauri.

Warrick's job would be to convince the Sorgast that the baths worked and wouldn't cause any damage to any of them. They had witnessed Redmond's panic attack when it was his turn in the baths, so the Sorgast certainly knew that it wasn't as benign as an experience as Warrick, Nabyla, and others were assuring them. Whenever the subject of the baths arose, especially when it was mentioned that their time was due, the Sorgast would hold hands and seek guid-

ance from the unseen space above their heads, to which
they would converse in their native tongue.

Warrick knew enough of the language to understand the
comments the Sorgast made. They were asking for direc-
tions from their elders. What mystified the crew was that
the Sorgast seemed to be getting answers. Whenever the
subject of the baths came up, however, the response from
the air apparently was controversial. The Sorgast's eyes
moved from spot to spot, as if following a heated discussion. Then their hands would drop, and they'd shake their
heads.

"So, what is the answer," Warrick asked.

"The elders have no answer," Asorg said. "They are
not of one thought. It is very confusing to them and the
Sorgast."

"What you are going to have to do," Warrick suggested,
"is to make a decision without their assistance. You will
have to decide."

That idea shattered the group. They drew close together
and huddled. They shuffled off to their quarters, a hodgepodge of unneeded equipment that resembled a cave. They
stayed there without comment for days, appearing only for
necessities, such as food and natural relief.

Warrick had wanted the Sorgast to be in the baths the
same time as himself. He argued that he and Sam had the
closest rapport with the Sorgast and would be able to maintain that relationship if they were in suspended animation
together. But he was thwarted by the Sorgast refusal to
enter the baths.

Nabyla was glad to separate the Sorgast and Warrick.
She wanted the aliens to meet and get to know other crew
members and understand differences between humans. She
only hoped they would recognize that Davis was a character
to himself. Fortunately Davis had a sexual fear of the aliens,
uncertain how Luba would react to Asorg if the Sorgast
made moves on her. So Davis kept his distance and insisted
that Luba do the same. For her part, Luba wanted Davis as
far away from Ranan as possible. Luba was small-breasted
and Ranan was marvelously full-figured, a fact not lost on
any of the women, nor the men, in the crew.

By and large the crew and the Sorgast melded well. The crew enjoyed showing the Sorgast the amazing tools of the twenty-second century. Sorgan was able to play video games within a few weeks of being introduced to them. In fact, he proved to have a dexterity that surpassed everyone else on board. Anderson dubbed him ''the pinball wizard from a strange planet.''

Warrick and Sam exited the baths room and were greeted by the crew. Asorg saw him, did a perfectly timed triple somersault, and gave Warrick a bear hug that the crew accepted as being the Sorgast ritual of greeting. After nearly splintering Warrick's ribs with his hug, Asorg stiffly stuck out his arm and pumped it vigorously as Warrick grasped his hand.

''Hello, old friend,'' Warrick said. ''You see I'm fine.''

Asorg contemplated Warrick; then turned his attention to Sam, who smiled and waved at him. He had seen them breathe in the fluids of the baths and watched them become unconscious and unseeing. He had visited the baths almost every day, throwing his body over their plastic containers and mumbling in his strange tongue. Now Asorg had to decide if his friends awoke because of his science or because of his incantations.

He recognized his dilemma. His friends had proved it was safe. Now even if the elders disagreed, he would have to take the chance himself or disgrace his protectors, friends, and companions. Asorg knew he had to do it. *Could it be worse than those darts?* he thought. He remembered the pain and the almost instant dizziness, fighting the fear that he would never see his mate or his child again. Now he would have to go through it all over again. The question in his mind, however, was whether Ranan and Sorgan would also let fluid in their lungs unless the elders approved. The elders had no experience in that; without experience they could not approve. Asorg could not breathe the fluids if his family didn't come with him. The elders could not help him for they did not know what suspended animation would do to the ability to contact people while they slept.

*   *   *

The calendar was kept by the spaceship computer, which didn't age and chugged along on Earth hours. It flashed 00: 00 010125.

"Happy New Year," Nabyla said to her empty state-room. According to the crew's calculations, the *Harley* was a mere 192 trillion miles from Earth, less than a light-year away. It was time to wake the crew and the aliens and start getting ready for the coast into the Solar System.

It was also time to rehearse what the crew was going to do when it got close enough to begin what Nabyla expected to be protracted negotiations with Earth authorities. Their constant monitoring of the radio reports both on military, commercial, and private industry bands showed that they were still the only people to have successfully brought an alien this close to Earth.

Nabyla, Redmond, and Davis had been assigned the task of informing Earth that the *Harley* and its crew were alive and well and on no one's authority but its own, the *Harley* had gone to Alpha Centauri, located some humanoids, and was bringing them back to Earth alive and well and speaking English.

Davis and Nabyla considered sending a coded message to Earth's civilian governments in order to begin negotiations for their safety and their rewards. They were certain that plenty of military types as well as some governments would battle for control of the aliens and their secrets, even though the aliens knew less about their planet than the first probes had discovered. The civilian governments would want to show how their citizens had produced a major accomplishment, or they might want to show they were going to enforce United Nations regulations against kidnapping humanoids wherever they existed in the Universe.

Redmond opposed the idea. Secret contacts would be hidden from the media or leaked for the benefit of governments, not the crew. If the return of the *Harley* was sent out on commercial networks, the *Harley* would be in control of information, not governments that had the power to make the *Harley* disappear for real.

Freedom of the press had achieved a life well beyond what Thomas Jefferson might have dreamed possible when he wrote the United States Constitution's Bill of Rights more than three hundred years before the *Harley*'s return. With the expansion of the Internet information superhighway, everyone with a computer could create his or her own home page, own information service, and own dissemination of news. It created a hodgepodge of networks, each serving a specific purpose. On-line newspapers were created in a twinkling of an input command and died just as quickly when billions of computer users ignored the ignoble and paid attention to the networks that delivered information.

Despite the free and rapid exchange of ideas on the Net, the seventeenth-century newspaper still existed. People around the world still needed something to read over the morning cup of coffee or other daily stimulant, still wanted to entertain themselves while holding a strap on the morning commuter rush, and still wanted something to read while on the toilet. Even the pervasive fax machine failed to beat the newspaper for advertisements. You could still reach a lot more people a lot less expensively by using a newspaper than you could using a fax or television or radio.

Redmond argued that by broadcasting openly that the *Harley* was coming home and that it had cooperative aliens on board, the governments, industry, and military would have to respond to the crew's presence, not hide it. "Certainly, they are going to send squadrons up here to off-load our cargo before we get to Earth, but the world will know we are alive and that Asorg, Ranan, and Sorgan exist, too," Redmond argued.

"And," he said with a twinkle in his eye, "imagine what kind of bidding war the tabloids will get into for an interview with us and the aliens. Think of the book deals. We'll have millions before we even get inside Jupiter's orbit."

Redmond smiled. Nabyla smiled. Davis smiled. Redmond's smile melted. "Of course, someone is going to have to go to the press conference." Redmond's eyes shifted toward Nabyla, the same direction that Davis's index finger was pointing.

13

THE CREW IS GRILLED BY THE MEDIA

THE SCREEN WENT WHITE AND THEN DARK AS THE LIGHTS in the room came up on command from the podium. Nabyla walked unsteadily to the lectern. She grabbed the wooden sides of the podium with both hands and forced air into her lungs.

"I'm Nabyla Guerrero Cohane, the captain of the DSV *Harley.*" She swallowed. "You've seen the film of our report to the government of the United States, the Secretariat of the United Nations, and the chairman of Space Control, Inc." She swallowed. "Are there any questions?"

The room exploded in noise, strobe lights, and shouted questions. Following centuries of protocol, she acknowledged the reporter from the Associated Press.

"Where are the aliens now?" she asked.

"The United Nations' authorities removed the Sorgast from the *Harley* when we passed the orbit of Mars. We have been told that the Sorgast—Asorg is the male, Ranan is the female, and Sorgan is their son—are being kept in quarantine for eight weeks until medical experts are con-

vinced that they harbor no viruses or bacteria that would
be detrimental to people on Earth. The Sorgast, as the family unit is known, are in the care of the U.N. authorities.
You should direct your questions toward those authorities
to determine the conditions of the Sorgast.

"By the way, you as journalists should be aware that the
Sorgast understand English and a smattering of other Earth
languages. They can read newspapers, and they have feel-
ings that are very similar to those of people born on Earth.
They would consider being referred to as 'aliens' as gross
an error as you being referred to as a 'wife.' "

There was a slight gasp as the reporters recoiled from
her use of the slur.

Then the horde screamed for attention and their questions, but the woman from AP pressed on. "A follow-up
question, Captain?" Nabyla nodded. "You lived with the
ali . . . Sorgast for eighteen years and you breathed the same
air they did; you ate the same foods; apparently you shook
their hands and gave them hugs; you shared tight living
quarters with them, yet none of you became ill and you and
your crew were not quarantined. Can you explain why?"

"Frankly, I cannot," Nabyla said, allowing anger to enter her voice and hoping the reporters would think she was
angry at the U.N. and not at the media. "I have to admit
that we were concerned that we would suffer some illnesses
that the Sorgast were immune to and vice versa. We inoculated the Sorgast when they came aboard the ship and
we believe that may have prevented them from falling ill
from the bacteria we carry. However, we had no protection
against any foreign viruses the Sorgast might carry.

"Our only choice would have been to isolate these people for the eighteen years it took to travel from their planet
to ours. We could not do that in good conscience."

Another reporter leaped to his feet and Nabyla recognized the UPI-Reuters newsman. "My sources indicate that
the reason the er . . . Sorgast were removed from your presence is that the authorities frankly do not believe your explanation of how they came to 'agree' to go aboard your
ship when you first encountered them. They were especially
concerned because all other reported contacts with human-

oids on Alpha Centauri have met with almost suicidal resistance and outright hostility.''

Nabyla hoped her hands were not betraying her. She could feel her nails dig into the veneer. ''I understand that there are some questions regarding our first meeting with the Sorgast and how we came to discuss their ascent to space, but I recognize that no one will believe us until you hear directly from the Sorgast themselves,'' Nabyla said, saying a prayer in her heart that the trio would stick to their well-rehearsed—the crew had instructed them what to say every day for eighteen months—lines.

''And,'' the pesky reporter continued, ''there are others who doubt whether the Sorgast are really aliens or are just an elaborate hoax created by you and the crew to explain your forty-year absence. Can you respond to that?''

''That's a very good question, Bryan. And it will be controversial for some time. Aside from their skin color, which is greenish and not a consequence of spaceship lighting, we were unable to discern any major or minor differences between the Sorgast and ourselves.'' A rumble went up in the crowd, and Nabyla picked out words that pertained to how closely did they examine each other. She held up her hand. ''I was getting to that. Many of you have been in space, but the vast majority of you have not and the vast majority of the people in the world,'' she deliberately picked out a hot camera and smiled broadly into it, ''have not gone into space. The first thing you have to deal with in space is the rather mundane problem of waste disposal.'' Laughter swept over the reporters as the meaning of her words struck home.

''The Sorgast had no knowledge of plumbing, no knowledge of technology, no knowledge of space travel, and certainly no idea how a space toilet works. We had to show them the proper use of space toilet facilities, and we didn't have time to spend a few weeks explaining the flushing mechanisms. We had to show them how we do it so they could do it. So we all had ample opportunity to recognize each other's operating parts.

''The crew of the *Harley*, myself, of course, included, recognized immediately how much alike we are. We did not have DNA-testing apparatus on the *Harley*, and I assume that one of the studies being done while the Sorgast are confined is DNA testing to determine exactly how close the Sorgast and humans are.

"I personally believe that if we are not brothers and sisters, we must be first cousins." Technicians noted where on their tape recorders and cameras that statement was made. Reporters scribbled religiously in their notebooks. Professional reporters knew a sound bite when they heard one.

"In fact," Nabyla said, "I think and predict that the Sorgast will be found to be so close to us genetically that they will be regarded as the same species biologically and perhaps a different race as sub-Saharan Africans differ from Chinese or Caucasians. The Sorgast, I think science will find, are simply green-skinned humans."

A chorus of questions again erupted from the thousand journalists crowded into the hangar at the Mideast Spaceport on the Egyptian-Israeli border—the site at which Nabyla, who had major roots in the area, insisted the conference be conducted.

"Let me continue a second," she said, loosening her grip on the podium. "As we came to realize that the Sorgast were nearly as human as the rest of the crew we understood that questions of authenticity would be hurled at us. We knew that we had taken a big risk and might be hunted as outlaws or at least thrown into jail as common thieves. I've had nightmares of digging for tungsten on Jupiter"—a murmur of chuckles awarded her attempt at humor.

"From the time the Sorgast were brought aboard the spacecraft until they were removed by United Nations agents two weeks ago, we recorded their every movement aboard the ship. We have a box of compressed CD-ROM discs which were write-protected by twelve different individuals with random codes to prevent those discs from being altered. Those are the original discs which will be presented to the Smithsonian Institution's Museum of Flight. Other sets will be presented to various museums on request."

Someone shouted from the back of the room. "For free?"

Nabyla smiled. "I didn't say that." As the room responded with laughter and more questions, Nabyla pointed to a television anchorperson, knowing that he already had a set question which she hoped would not have anything to do with money.

"The Sorgast are primitive people," he intoned. "Do you believe that you have upset their way of life by taking them from pre–Stone Age development to the Interstellar Era in just a few minutes of time? Are we doing something unnatural?"

Thank God for television, Nabyla said to herself. An ethical-sociological discussion was far more safe than trying to explain how they bludgeoned poor Asorg into the suspended-animation pools or how Sorgan suffered a stubborn infection for a couple of weeks from where he was stuck with Nabyla's dart.

"Of course," Nabyla said, "we don't believe that we have done anything wrong. The Sorgast are highly intelligent, remarkably dexterous people. They have a high sense of purpose as individuals; they have maintained a very strong family unit over the eighteen years we have known them—although a spaceship is a weird laboratory for testing acclimatization to a new society. They have maintained their own ceremonies, some of which seem to be of a highly religious nature. I don't think that I personally would be a person who, having the ability to help people—people like myself—could leave them to suffer the consequences of life on Alpha Centauri. Life is brutal there. Death is ever-present and can attack from above, on the ground, and from under the soil.

"I think we should remove all the people from that planet and bring them to safety and bring them up-to-date on the progress of humanity. I think it would have been criminal of us to have seen the predicament of the Sorgast and not offered to help them. Now, others—anthropologists, sociologists, and others—may disagree, but that is how I felt, and my crew felt the same way."

"So," the reporter continued, "you see yourselves as some sort of interstellar rescue service?"

The edge to the question was apparent, and Nabyla expected it. "No," she said, "we really see ourselves as the same type of explorers that went out from Europe in the fifteenth and sixteenth centuries: looking for adventure and hopeful of finding something lucrative as well as hopeful of returning with our lives and bodies intact. We are not altruists, but we have come to empathize with the plight of the Sorgast."

Nabyla pointed to an outrageously coifed woman in the middle of the room. "Can you tell us how you fared in negotiations with the various governments and industrial powers you've had to deal with—and I'm particularly interested in how much money you made from this escapade?"

There was nervous laughter in the room. Nabyla said, "Let me begin to answer that question by telling you that certain aspects of the negotiations are sealed—which means they can't leave my lips, but I'm sure you all have sources that can pry the information out of someone.

"Legally, the major concern was how SCI was going to respond to a forty-year unauthorized rental of their equipment, notably the *Harley*. We told the company litigators that we would not press for back pay" (hearty laughter) "if they would not press criminal charges."

She paused. "Actually, you should all realize that was a joke. SCI recognized that there was a great deal of scientific and proprietary information we could provide about our voyage; the steps we took in scheduling animated suspension baths to assure that we all would not show our forty years in space. I went into space when I was twenty-six. I was born in 2061. That would mean today, in 2127, I'm sixty-six years old. But, I think you'd agree that I don't look like someone who has spent sixty-six years on this planet. That's because I've spent more than thirty years in suspended animation.

"SCI wanted to secure information of that nature. We were able to create a few technical revisions to radio transmissions and other technical matters. The company was also anxious to retrieve and maintain the maps we made of objects we saw in deep space during the journey. A company executive said that the information we had accrued during the trip was invaluable to SCI and more than assuaged their corporate anger at having spent a few hundred million searching for us and the additional expense of having to send another ship to patrol the area we vacated.

"We were happy to avoid prosecution. They were pleased with the unique information we could provide.

"The United Nations, as you know from the press reports from the Secretariat, wanted us drawn and quartered" (laughter) "and that was just the start" (more laughter). "The position of the international organization, as it was explained to us, was that we had seriously violated the interstellar laws made to protect developing humanoids. Frankly the UN officials said they didn't believe our story on how the humanoids came to join us on this mission and accused us of kidnapping and suggested we had probably killed dozens of Sorgast before capturing the three that returned to Earth with us.

"I have to say that negotiations were very difficult and very sharp. I believe that if you—the world's news media—had not been alerted and were not pressing for details about this story, I can conceive of us being simply blown out of an airlock somewhere between here and Mars."

Nervous chuckles were scattered throughout the hangar. "But when the UN stopped being angry and we stopped being defensive, we were able to accomplish some major negotiations. The UN decided not to prosecute us—if the Sorgast backed up our contention that they had not been forcibly removed from the planet or if the Sorgast refused to demand prosecution—provided that we hand over to the UN our detailed records of how we learned the Sorgast speech and what our observations of them were. We decided that was a deal we could make in the interests of interstellar harmony. The UN, for its part, promised to produce a Sorgast language dictionary and also to reserve a seat for the Sorgast in the UN if the planet's population ever sought such a seat."

Nabyla poured water into a glass, the ice clinking. A

couple of drops splattered out. She wiped them up with a napkin.

"Now the next group we had to deal with was the United States."

An impertinent reporter yelled out, "Why the U.S.? They have no authority in space."

Nabyla smiled. "No, they don't. But that's beside the point" (a few snickers). "The position of the U.S., I guess, is that they are the U.S., and therefore they have an interest. We did not feel that we were in a position to argue.

"The U.S. stated that their only interest was in scientific, especially medical, analysis of the Sorgast to determine if they were a threat to the population because of microorganisms that might be contained in their bodies.

"The U.S. also wanted to do DNA studies to eliminate the possibility of fraud: Our DNA is on record, so by comparing the DNA of the Sorgast to ours they could determine if the Sorgast were really our offspring, genetically engineered to have a different-colored skin. I digress here a minute to explain that while we have the knowledge and ability to do what was suggested, we did not have the equipment aboard the *Harley* to accomplish this. Nevertheless, had the U.S. authorities not demanded that they do this test, we would have asked them to do it. We need proof that the Sorgast are from another planet.

"The U.S. also wants to do sophisticated DNA tests to determine how closely the Sorgast are related to Homo sapiens.

"We did not object to any of these scientific studies being done as long as we could be assured, and as long as the Sorgast were assured, that they would not have to undergo any experiments that involved consciousness-altering procedures. We—and when I say 'we' in this context I am talking about the crew and the Sorgast—had no objections to blood or saliva being examined or having the Sorgast undergo noninvasive diagnostic-imaging studies. The Sorgast were adamant that they not be given drugs that could interfere with their religious ceremonies, in which they go into a trancelike séances. We received assurances that they would not be maltreated while they were confined for two months." *Nor*, Nabyla added to herself, *will they be given truth serum drugs that would reveal the truth of how they were captured.*

"We were assured that in return for their cooperation the Sorgast would receive U.S. government assistance in resettling on Earth, including protection from the overly curious—and," Nabyla smiled, "those journalists who don't have contracts for interviews (laughter, mixed with a number of grumbles). The U.S. also said that for our cooperation, the government would not prosecute us."

The same reporter shouted, "What grounds could they have prosecuted on?" Other reporters asked the same.

Nabyla paused to collect her thoughts and to make sure she wouldn't say anything that could result in a premature accidental death. "We were assured that U.S. laws had been violated, but inasmuch as we were cooperating with the authorities, there would be no reason to use the heavy hand of justice. The U.S. position has been—and you should ask the president herself—that the arrival of the Sorgast on Earth could prove to be the greatest event in the history of mankind.

"Those of us who have studied history remember that Christopher Columbus, after discovering the New World, spent the rest of his life barely able to avoid being jailed because of debts racked up on those historic trips. I think the authorities would desire to avoid the same tarnishing of a marvelous event. Certainly we would appreciate that as well."

Nabyla took a sip from the glass and let her tongue moisten her lips, an act that caused more than one male reporter to feel his heart miss a couple of beats.

"Personally, I dare say that we all will fare quite well from this coup of bringing the Sorgast to Earth. I think we are all booked for interviews for the next six months, and I'm not unhappy to report that we, indeed, will be paid for those interviews. I apologize to those who object to checkbook journalism, but we have information and it's for sale. I have been approached by several publishing houses to write about the trip, and I know that the Sorgast have also

FOR THE COMING MILLENNIUM****

been approached and they are willing to tell their story as
well.''

Her eyes twinkled, and a smile crossed her face. ''However, the Sorgast still have a long way to go in their knowledge of English, so it's likely they will need a coauthor. I
can give anyone who is interested the name of the agent
handling such requests after the news conference,'' she
said, noting with satisfaction a number of eager expressions
in the crowd.

She continued. ''We went to Alpha Centauri seeking
wealth and fame, and I think we are going to achieve that.
I hope we can handle those twin icons of capitalism well,
but we are a diverse group.''

A sea of hands went up and reporters shouted for recognition. Nabyla spotted a primly dressed man about ten
rows back and signaled to him for the question.

''Thank you, I'm Jonathan Mason of *Christian World
News*,'' he began as several sighs and groans escaped from
others, ''and my readers want to know how human beings
could live on two different solar systems if the Bible states
that people on Earth are the Chosen People of God?''

The room tittered. Nabyla smiled, thankful to get into an
area where she only had to give her opinion and not worry
about facts. The fewer facts she gave away in the press
conference meant the more facts that she could include in
her book, her television series, her television talk shows,
her movies, etc.

''Mr. Mason, as you can appreciate, I am not a theologian, although all the members of the crew have some understanding of theology through our classes in the Space
Academy. Those classes, as I'm sure you know, help us
deal with the religious preferences and ideologies of other
crew members. Since people will spend decades in space
together, it is necessary to have some understanding of their
religious ceremonies to avoid faux pas which could upset
the chemistry of a space crew.

''But I'm assuming you recognize my shortcomings as
a student of divinity and you are actually wondering about
my opinion on the nature of this phenomenon, if indeed
the Sorgast are determined to be human beings. They cer-

tainly look human, sound human, act human, but until DNA studies and MRI studies are completed we won't know if they are human. Is that what you are asking?''

Mason affirmed her statement with a nod.

''Let me tell you, Mr. Mason, and the rest of you, that we as a crew seriously considered the consequences on religious thought that the discovery of the Sorgast will have because it will play havoc with some religions. There are many ways to explain the presence of human beings on other planets in other solar systems, but only a few make any sense at all.

''We considered the possibility that we were not the first to visit Alpha Centauri. Is it possible that hundreds of thousands of years ago there flourished on Earth a civilization so advanced that it had perfected interstellar travel? If there was such a civilization, is it not possible that members of that human society ventured into space and founded this colony on Alpha Centauri, and then abandoned it there because of harsh conditions? The colonists survived, but cut off from home supplies, the colony could only flourish over the generations as a cave society.

''We thought long and hard about that scenario, and we rejected it. First, there is no solid evidence on Earth that such an advanced society existed, although some people will point to the pyramids in Egypt or stone carvings in Mayan temples or other phenomena around the world as evidence of visits or the development of an advanced society. Where are the space launch facility ruins; where are the highways that would have been necessary for such a society to engage in commerce? This evidence doesn't exist. Secondly, the Sorgast have no knowledge at all of an ancient colony. One would think that if such a colony existed it would be remembered at least as a legend. Our discussions with the Sorgast revealed nothing of that nature.

''So we discounted the possibility that Earthlings seeded the colony on Alpha Centauri.

''Then we considered the possibility of just a fabulous coincidence that evolution on Alpha Centauri was similar to evolution on Earth and the human form which combines dexterity and intelligence is a natural survivor among the zillions of combinations of genes that Mother Nature can put together. But you've all seen the creatures that inhabit the Sorgast's planet. These are creatures that we couldn't conjure up in a nightmare. So why would we be able to find intelligent life—at least intelligent in the human sense—on this planet, intelligent life that looks like mirror images of ourselves? One would expect an intelligent form with a half dozen eyes, placed strategically around the body; limbs more like tentacles; or something along those lines. I'm sure we could all come up with a more effective intelligence wedded to a better-functioning body if we were the Creator.

"So we rejected that idea, too. I have to tell you, members of the media, that we didn't just discuss these ideas for fifteen minutes. There were years of cumulative thought and discussion and some heated arguments that went into these talks among ourselves. You have to remember that when you are traveling through space in computer-operated ships, the only thing you have to do is make sure the blinking lights stay on. It can be boring, so these discussions were lively, well documented from our voluminous data storage facilities, and well thought out. After you've seen *Casablanca* twenty times and everyone on the crew can beat Bogart to Rick's lines, you are more than willing to engage in intellectual jousting."

Again Nabyla paused. She wondered how long it would be before the television networks had to leave the live conference and cover the latest bridge disaster, or when the newspaper reporters would have to leave to write for the next edition. She was relaxed and, as she sipped the water again, realized she was having fun being a spokesperson.

She scanned the crowd again, but couldn't discern anyone getting antsy yet. The strobe lights continue to flash intermittently. She wondered, *How many different pictures of me can they take?*

She inhaled deeply. "The two best scenarios that we came up with were these. First, and most simple. God is Great and if He—or She," Nabyla said with emphasis and a smile, "wanted to create humans on several different planets simultaneously, it certainly would be in God's power to do so if we believe that God did create the world and the Universe. There are Biblical scholars who believe that the Bible refers to previous civilizations that God abandoned because they didn't work out the way God thought they would. So perhaps it is possible that God's hand created the Sorgast as well as humans.

"We could not dismiss this argument, because if we accept God as all-powerful then there is no reason not to accept that God could have created both races with the snap of His or Her fingers. To accept this version all you must do is believe in the power of the Almighty. And frankly many members of the crew had no trouble accepting this explanation. All it takes is faith."

Nabyla watched Mason scribbling furiously in his notebook. He also had a tape recorder digitizing her words, but like most reporters, notes became stories first and then were sometimes rechecked by the recordings. Nabyla knew some reporters who said they never listened to any of the hours of tapes they recorded, and no one had ever accused them of misquotation in a story. She paused long enough for Mason to finish writing and waited for his eyes to seek hers again.

She went on. "There is another explanation." She stopped for effect. "It is an explanation that I, as a practical scientist, somehow believe truly explains the existence of a humanlike race on a planet near to another humanlike race.

"I think, and of course I can't prove this now but the DNA tests may help us with this determination, that the Sorgast and we humans have the same fathers."

A puzzled stir arose from the reporters.

"Stay with me on this," she exhorted. "What if a hundred thousand years ago, a million years ago, ten million years ago—not a terribly long time in the fifteen-billion-year-old Universe—there arose on a distant star or galaxy, an advanced civilization capable of spaceflight? What if this civilization, judging itself to being the most advanced society in the Universe, sent missionaries throughout the galaxies to find livable colonies on distant stars? What if when they found livable planets that had the proper atmosphere and relationship to the star at the center of that solar system, they began searching for intelligent creatures? What if when they found those creatures they captured them and basically raped them with gene-altering DNA which resulted in this intelligent life having the opportunity to become the dominant form on that planet?

"Anthropologists on Earth are still confused over the sudden change in Homo erectus that created two branches of near humans—those that eventually became Cro-Magnon or modern man and those that were Neandertals. Around 300,000 years ago, even though Neandertal man was dominant, he slowly disappeared and Cro-Magnon emerged triumphant. The question has been: What gave Cro-Magnon the advantage over Neandertal? We think it could have been the impregnation of certain Neandertals with genes from this 'fly-by-night' intergalactic colonizer.

"How will we know if we are correct? Well, the first clues could come from the Tau Ceti mission. If that group finds humanlike creatures, and there is another DNA match, then I think we will have to consider than maybe we are all Children of the Aliens, and none of us really live on a home planet. In fact, we may never even know what our home planet is."

There was a profound silence, but a silence that lasted only seconds.

"Why," shouted the reporter from *National Geographic*, "isn't it possible that under your last hypothesis that the original alien race could have taken Cro-Magnon from Earth and redeposited him elsewhere?"

"That's a good question," Nabyla said, "an interesting hypothesis, and I'm afraid I can't give a good answer. It is possible that it happened that way."

A man with a British accent got her attention, "Ian West, the *Galactic Enquirer*. Could it not be that reports through the last few decades of abduction by aliens are actually repressed memories of what happened hundreds of thousands of years ago that resurface because of some form of stimulus in people today?"

Nabyla smiled, visualizing the headlines. "I think that

might possibly be an explanation for some of those reports," she said diplomatically.

For the next dozen of questions, Nabyla fielded a series of questions formulated around individual reporters' on-the-spot theories of evolution and development, which she deftly handled by simply agreeing that what was being proposed had some possibility of being true. Nabyla was pleased with her job. No one was trying to pin her down on how the Sorgast were captured, the crew's biggest legal problem, nor how much money they were making. Nabyla knew that not everything was being split down the middle. Some of the crew members were better interviewees; some had better agents. *We are all going to be rich,* Nabyla mused, *but some are going to be richer than others.*

When the disparities in worth were finally figured out, would there be someone in the group who would spill the beans? How long could a group of people be quiet? She thought back to her history lessons and remembered the "Boiler Room girls" who worked for Senator Robert F. Kennedy in his campaign for president that resulted in his assassination in 1968. A year later the girls and fellow workers, including Senator Edward M. Kennedy, got together on Chappaquiddick Island on Martha's Vineyard, a get-together that cost Mary Jo Kopechne her life. There were eight other women who were at that party. All went to their deaths between fifty and seventy-five years later without ever revealing a word about what happened that night. Not even in their wills or in their personal notes was there an accounting of the event. *So,* Nabyla thought, *there is hope we can keep this secret, too.*

The woman representing the *Wall Street Journal,* a strange name for a financial paper considering that there were no longer any stock markets on Wall Street—a casualty of the information superhighway and the ability to transact trades over the Internet, tried to get the questioning back to comments on facts. The press conference was already more than an hour and a half old, and most of the reporters had their stories. This reporter was looking for details.

"You refer to the people of the Alpha Centauri planet as Sorgast. But does that term represent all the people of the planet or just this family unit or the clan in which they live?"

"From what we were able to learn from Asorg and Ranan, the Sorgast is the name for their community group, which I believe we estimated to be about twenty-five to thirty people. Asorg said there are other human groups on the planet because he has seen them in the distance and occasionally a member of another group would stagger into the Sorgast area in a search for food or because the person was lost.

"You have to remember that this planet is so hostile that attempts to cross a wide area can result in a wide variety of attacks from creatures that move far faster than the Sorgast. Basically, people try to remain in their own enclave, where there is enough food and water to maintain a semblance of life and livelihood.

"To answer your question: The Sorgast are certainly this family unit; and most likely it is the name for the clan. It could be the name for all the humanoids on the planet. Asorg and Ranan, in our discussions on board the *Harley*, indicated no particular physical differences among the clans, aside from different shades of green. They apparently differ from an olivelike color to an almost aquamarine. From the way Asorg talked, and he had most of the encounters with other clans, the coloring tended to help camouflage the Sorgast. Those that lived in forest areas, such as Asorg's family, were a darker shade of green; those who lived near bodies of water had lighter, brighter skin colors."

Nabyla noticed that several of the reporters had left and a couple of camera crews had turned off their machines. She was flagging a bit. She refilled her glass.

Mason was politely raising his hand again, and Nabyla recognized him.

"Mr. Mason?"

The reporter beamed and colored, surprised that he would be remembered by name amid the sea of journalists.

"Captain," he asked formerly, "there has been mention

of strange séancelike sessions the Sorgast conducted which,
I believe, were considered almost religious-like among your
crew. Can you give us more of an idea about those sessions?''

Nabyla had wanted to keep that information private, but
she felt she had the press on her side now and didn't want
to antagonize anyone.

Her grandfather was a U.S. senator, and he always told
her that if a reporter thinks you are telling the truth, he'll
give you the benefit of the doubt. But if he even suspects
that you are trying to be tricky, he'll hound you to the end
of time. Nabyla remembered her grandfather telling her the
apocryphal tale of ''his pappy.'' ''My pappy always said,''
her grandfather related, ''you never get in a pissing match
with a fellow who buys ink by the boxcar load.'' Since
Nabyla's grandfather was a Harvard graduate, as was his
father, Nabyla knew he was more likely referred to as ''sir''
rather than ''Pappy,'' but she understood the message.

She stared at Mason and told him about the Sorgast's
ceremonies. ''They would gather in a circle and hold hands
and after saying a few prayers—or what we then assumed
were prayers but later found out were simple relaxation,
trance-inducing tones—mantras, I guess—they would suddenly begin talking.

''We were mystified by these séances because it seemed
as if the Sorgast were having a conversation with something
ethereal. We couldn't see anything, but it was obvious they
could, and they seemed to be getting answers from whatever it was they were seeing.''

The audience was silent, stunningly so, thought Nabyla.

''When we had learned enough about the Sorgast language, and we had their confidence that we were friends
and meant them no harm, they eventually opened up to us
about these séances. I think their reluctance at first to discuss this aspect of their lives with us was due to a feeling
that we were mocking them. In fact, we later learned that
they could not believe that we did not commune with our
elders.

''Here's what we know about the Sorgast and their ceremonies. They can concentrate strongly enough to excite

certain brain waves which put them in a soft trance. While in that trance they can visualize former members of their family unit or clan who have died. Except the Sorgast have no word for death. For them, everyone who ceases to live and breathe and move on their planet simply passes into another dimension. The Sorgast say that they can communicate with these people—their elders they call them, sometimes including children—to the point where they can ask questions and get answers. The Sorgast said it was communication with the elders that made them realize that we were friendly and meant no harm.

"Frankly, I wish I could tell you more about this communication with the dead—that's the way I look at it, but that is something that the Sorgast know more about than I. They seemed open about it with us, so I believe that when their social and language skills improve we will be able to understand a great deal more about this unique ability."

Nabyla fielded a few more questions about the Sorgast and their elders, but begged off, saying her knowledge was limited. The elders, Nabyla knew, were going to be a main part of her book. The Sorgast, after six years of intense study while awake and after receiving subliminal language lessons for twelve years in the baths, spoke English like Oxford deans, but Nabyla wanted to try and maintain a bit of mystery about them for purely personal economic reasons.

With the press conference pushing two hours, Nabyla signaled to one of the NASA officials running the press conference that she had had enough. The one last question came from a television crew, which simply repeated some of the information she told Mason, but this time she was looking into the camera and knew that when it aired it would seem as if the pretty-faced anchorperson had been asking the pertinent questions instead of pirating them from another reporter. But that was the nature of the game. Nabyla felt relieved when it was over. She had swum with the sharks and still had all twenty digits.

14

THE ALIENS GET TO TELL THEIR STORY

ASORG HAD STRUGGLED WITH THE MATTER FOR MONTHS now that he was on Earth. He had consulted with Ranan, and he'd consulted with the elders, and the general feeling was that it was up to Asorg to make the final decision: Should he tell the world that he was shot, kidnapped, drugged, bound, and carried onto the spaceship without so much as a question, or should he do as Nabyla and Redmond and Davis beseeched them to do: lie through his teeth.

It hadn't been difficult to lie to the U.N. and U.S. authorities. They were so brutish and pompous and officious that Asorg enjoyed playing with them. They were so eager to punish the *Harley* crew that Asorg and Ranan immediately decided to play the game as Nabyla prayed they would.

"Yes, we encountered the crew about dusk and through hand signals they were able to make it known that they wanted us to travel with them to the stars. We agreed. They said we would have to be made to sleep so our journey would not be difficult, and we agreed to that as well. We understand that there is little likelihood we can ever return to our home, but if this new Earth is as wonderful a place as the *Harley* says, we would be happy to reside there and we would, of course, undergo testing to make sure we harbor no disease," Asorg told the U.N. authorities.

Ranan told U.S. authorities almost exactly the same thing. So precise was her description that the U.S. investigators were sure it was perfectly rehearsed. When they asked Sorgan the same questions, the child, now chronologically twenty-two, but physically just nine years old, described in marvelous details the first encounter, the difficulties in making each other understand their sign languages, the harrowing escapes from strange beasts. He went on and on and on, fabricating one anecdote after another, fully convincing the skeptics that the Sorgast made their own decision about boarding that spaceship that would whisk them away to another place.

Now Asorg was going to have to tell the world about what happened, and his insides churned. He knew he would continue the fiction. "Keep it simple," Nabyla had told him. "The press is interested in you and your planet. They won't nitpick about how you got on the ship. Everyone wants this to be aboveboard and legal. Remember, if you tell them you are dissatisfied, someone may decide that you and Ranan and Sorgan should be returned to your home planet. I'm not sure if you want that."

After three months on Earth, Asorg wanted nothing more than to explore this wonderful sphere in which people—creatures like himself—ruled without fear from creatures in the air or on the ground. He found it considerably strange to have to worry about whether human beings would attack him rather than being concerned about animal attacks. His family roared with laughter when he saw film clips in which people were terrified of roaches, mosquitoes, and rats. "If we only had to fear these pests, I would go back to Alpha Centauri tomorrow," he told his interrogators.

The U.S. authorities who were holding him and his family in special quarters in Roswell, New Mexico, finally agreed to constant media pressure for a press conference,

even though most of the studies, including the critical DNA
tests, had not been fully scrutinized.

The press conference was scheduled for the Santa Fe
Convention Center to allow for the 19,542 accredited members of the press to attend. Virtually every media outlet in
the world and even the fledgling journals from the Moon
and Mars made the incredibly expensive trip to Earth for
the event. Thousands more journalists were connected
through computer access or by telephone or television. It
was the most eagerly awaited news conference in the history of mankind.

After a fifteen-minute introduction, which included comments on the DNA testing being done, the Sorgast were
introduced. Asorg was shaking. He approached the podium
with a piece of paper in his hand. He placed it on the podium and deliberately smoothed it flat. The paper read, in
Nabyla's handwriting: "If the question bothers you or dis-
turbs you or surprises you, ask the reporter to repeat it. Ask
him to change the wording because you don't understand
what he is saying." Asorg understood English very well,
including tens of thousands of native idioms, but the audience just knew that he had learned the language on his
way to Earth and would forgive him if he had trouble understanding. At least that's what Nabyla had said.

He gazed out at the group. "Hello," he said slowly, carefully pronouncing each syllable. "My name is Asorg, and
I come from the planet near the star you call Alpha Centauri." He waited.

"I assume," he held his arms wide and then used his
hand as a visor to view beyond the first dozen rows where
the cameras were, "that you are what my friends from the
Harley call 'pack journalism.' "

The center almost jumped as the thousands of reporters
howled at the cleverness of the remark, which caught them
off guard.

"Under the rules of this session, I will be selecting numbers at random and those numbers will correspond to individual reporters. I will call the number, you will identify
yourself, and you will ask a question. I am asked by the
U.S. military authorities to say in public that no one knows

what question will be asked except for the person asking that question.

"We will start with number"—he reached into a circulating tub, and extracted a yellow plastic button—"289. Two Eight Nine."

A woman in the first deck leaped to her feet, shouting, "Yesss." "I'm Andrea Carlson of the *Denver Post*. Asorg of the Sorgast," she said, attempting to be formal, "tell us about life on your planet. What is the name of your planet, your sun, and what are your daily activities?"

Asorg exhaled. *Softball,* he said to himself, expecting that he could hear a nervous Nabyla saying the same thing to herself in Gaza City. "It is interesting that you ask me the name of my planet because in our language our planet roughly translates to Earth. We call our planet Earth as you call this planet Earth. You call our sun Alpha Centauri, we call our sun—the primary one—Life Bringer, and the secondary one—Light Bringer, because we see it more often. We do not have a word for your sun because we never knew it existed until we were in space. Your sun is in the part of the sky which the Sorgast never viewed in our home area.

"Our daily activity involves the never-ending hunt for food. There are numerous berries and fruits in the forest where we have our cave, but we, like you, are a carnivorous people and we require meats for sustenance. In that regard we seek the remains of carcasses left over when the giant creatures of our Earth fight among themselves. We do not have the amazing weaponry of your people, which would make life on our planet easier.

"I was astounded by how much people on Earth understand about their planet, their history, the functioning of their bodies as well as those of the creatures who live here in peace with you. We know so little compared to you. The most we know comes from our elders, with whom we convene daily, sometimes several times a day. The elders travel safely on the planet and can alert us to danger and the location of danger"—except, he thought ruefully, of dangers the elders knew nothing about such as tranquilizing darts—"and tell us where to hunt and when to hide."

He stopped abruptly and picked up another button: "One thousand forty-seven." There was a long pause, and finally a man wearing headphones stood up and raised his hand. He spoke in Japanese, announcing that he was a reporter for the Japanese national radio network. Asorg and twenty thousand other people put on headphones and listened as the simultaneous translator delivered the question, a follow-up on the roles of the elders. "Are the elders of whom you speak alive or are they spirits with whom you have contact?"

Asorg took advantage of the hesitation in the voice of the translator to ask for a confirmation of the question. The question was repeated.

"Before I try to answer that interesting question," he said, "let me tell you how very surprised I was to find out that the people of Earth speak so many different languages. The only others from outside our clan on our planet whom we have met all speak the same tongue, no matter if there are differences in skin tone or facial features or hair color. I marvel at the amazing diversity of language here.

"As to your inquiry about the elders. In your experience, I would assume you would say that we are speaking to spirits, apparitions, or ghosts. We do not refer to them in that way because these are forms of friends and relatives with whom we have lived for years. We speak directly to our elders, who have traveled with us from our planet. They traveled with us on the ship and they are here in the gracious quarters your government has provided for us in Roswell. They are alive to us, although we cannot embrace them physically. It is strange to Ranan and Sorgan and me that people on this planet do not have contact with elders. Perhaps your contact with them is in the works of literature and art and film that they leave behind, but, as my precocious son has observed, you do not have interactive relationships with your elders as we do.

"Your scientists were quite interested in this ability to talk to elders, especially since they cannot speak to them or see them or hear them, even though we know very well that they are present. Some of the scientists say that this ability may make us a different species of beings. I do not have the answer to that, except that I can see no difference between us and you. So I have to ask you the question: Perhaps you do not call upon your elders as we do, and therefore you cannot see them or hear them as we do. I think you should try to visit your elders because they are an unending source of help in living from day to day.''

Asorg dipped into the bin again, ignoring the Japanese journalist's attempt at a follow-up question. He appreciated Nabyla's suggestion as to how to run the press conference. It disrupted the flow of questions and made it difficult for the reporters to get a cohesive stream of questions together. Every reporter had his or her own priority and that took precedence over follow-up questions. Asorg's ignorance of press-conference procedures would allow him to dump follow-up questions which could prove sticky.

He called the next number and a man from a Vancouver, Columbia, formerly British Columbia, broadcasting station asked: ''We understand that you will be residing on this planet. Have you made any decisions as to where you will live?''

Asorg brightened. ''We have not selected a place to live yet, but it must be close to a hospital. This is—I think you call it—a scoop. Since our arrival here Ranan has conceived, and in 187 of your days, according to the calculations of the elders, we will present to the planet a new life, our daughter. Ranas.''

The room erupted in cheers, applause, and the scratching of ten thousand pens on paper.

Asorg continued. ''So we will be seeking a community that's a good place to raise children; that has good schools and day-care facilities. We are seeking a community which is similar to our climate, which would be dry but fertile with trees, water, and greenery. There are some areas of the state of Texas that are appealing. But we will not make a decision until after we complete a tour of your planet during the next few months.

''I have been told that even with this worldwide tour I will be able to earn monetary credits by speaking to various groups about comparisons between this Earth and my Earth. I have eighteen years of experiences aboard the *Harley* and twenty years of experiences on my planet to discuss. So at an hour or two a session, I hope I should never become boring or redundant.

"People have asked me if I feel homesick for my Earth. There are times I look into your heavens and am surprised to see but one sun. The temperature variability is also a surprise. On my world, there is little change. Perhaps that is because I am only familiar with certain areas of my planet, whereas you have completely explored your planet from pole to pole. It is nice to be able to walk outside on this world and not have to be on guard for an unprovoked attack from the sky or the ground.

"I like it here. Ranan is entranced with this planet, and Sorgan, who does not remember his home planet well at all, considers Earth his home. The U.S. government has asked us if we would like to receive citizenship here, and we are most likely to accept that, but we've asked to be allowed to make that decision following our tour of the rest of the major political divisions."

Asorg called several more numbers and fielded questions that were already known or could not yet be answered. The next number belonged to a reporter for the *New York Times*, and it was the question that Asorg feared the most.

"There have been rumors that you and your family were not as willing participants in the trip to Earth as the crew of the *Harley* suggested. Can you tell us about your impressions of your meeting and subsequent decision to come to Earth?"

"I'm not sure I understand your question. Are you asking for our viewpoint on the first meeting with Nabyla and her fellow crew members?"

The reporter started to change the focus of the statement again, but shrugged and nodded in agreement.

"It was a day, as I've said, like most days we experienced there. It was dry and comfortable. We were able to leave our sanctuary in the forest in our usual loincloths. We stepped beyond the edge of the forest in search of dead or dying animals nearby. We moved very slowly because the dangerous creatures on our planet are attracted by movement. We also ventured out at dusk because the flying creatures do not soar at night. We do not know why.'' Asorg paused and thought to himself, *And then the world went blank and I was awakened in shackles, floating around on a spaceship.*

He returned to his audience. ''I saw a strange movement on the surface. It was some kind of creature, I thought, but it moved at phenomenal speed and suddenly stopped between us and the forest. I feared the movement would attract the ground creatures and I was frightened when the side of the vehicle—although I still called it a creature in my mind—opened and out stepped Nabyla. I didn't know it was Nabyla, just that it was a female person. She held what I believe was a weapon in her hand. I had my spear but I knew that whatever she was holding was certainly more powerful than my spear if she could control a creature that could move so quickly and quietly.''

Asorg paused a second to contemplate what to say next. So far his fabrication sounded good. It was fairly close to what he had told investigators. ''Keep lies simple,'' Davis had told him. ''It's easier to remember them that way.''

Asorg had rehearsed in his mind the answer to this question so many times that it almost started to seem real to him. He had asked the elders for help and they had provided a number of details. They seemed to be in favor of the fraud, although there were some dissidents in the ethereal assembly.

He chuckled out loud. ''I recall being mystified by this woman who was talking rapidly in a language that made no sense to me, but I was also worried about Ranan and Sorgan. She began drawing figures in the ground, and pointing to the sky. It made no sense to me: How could people come from the sky? I made signs to indicate that I didn't believe her, and she made signs indicating that she could show us what she meant. She spoke into her hand and almost instantly a huge creature appeared in the sky and settled to the ground within ten yards of us.

''Our astonishment froze us in place. We had to be almost carried on board we were so stunned. On board we were placed in front of a screen which showed us pictures of what was to happen next. I was impressed that Davis was able to use a handheld device—a type of computer-camera—to transfer our images to the screen and show us what we were going to be doing. I was concerned about the injections we had to receive to protect us against thrashing about during the powerful thrust into space and to protect us against spacesickness.''

Asorg reached for another number, but the *Times* reporter was quickly on his feet. "Please, Asorg of Sorgast, tell us: Did you go into that Space Shuttle because you were curious or because you were threatened by the weaponry being displayed by the *Harley* crew?"

There was a serious edge to the man's voice, and Asorg knew his answer was critical. In truth, of course, he and his family were unconscious, but that answer wouldn't work now. "We, certainly I, was more curious than afraid. And once we saw the remarkable devices on the shuttle we were anxious to see more and experience more. Also we had an idea of what was happening from conversations with our elders and from visits from other clans who had told what we considered tall tales of visitors from the sky—recent stories.

"Curiosity killed the cat, you say here on Earth. Curiosity has opened a whole world to us."

Back in Gaza City, Nabyla and Redmond leaped into each other's arms and spilled champagne as they toasted Asorg. They were not going to jail after all, and they would be able to live like millionaires.

Asorg called out a five-digit number and an Aukland tabloid journalist asked, "You have been very positive about your trek to this planet. Can you tell us some of the negative things about the trip?"

"The baths. The baths were the worst thing. I still shudder when I think of them. I don't know how I got through them. Actually I do know, I was drugged, bludgeoned, and drowned against my will." There was rustling and mumbling among the crowd, and Asorg realized that he might have experienced something most of the people in the audience knew nothing about.

He waited briefly. "I get the feeling that many of you

are not familiar with what I mean about the baths. Is that true?''

A chorus of affirmation was heard.

''I'm not talking about cleansing rooms where sonic waves were able to remove soil and oils and disinfect, but the suspended-animation baths. I was in space for eighteen years which could mean that I am about forty of your Earth years old. The orbital cycle on my planet is similar to yours but maybe a few weeks longer. But anyway, I don't look like a forty-year-old because twelve of the years en route here I was in the baths, in suspended animation.

''In order to go into suspended animation you have to lie down in this gelatin-like tube and be immersed in fluid. Where I grew up, you didn't dive into water from a pond and try to breathe. If you did that you became an elder; you passed into another dimension. You would say that such a person died.

''In space, however, this fluid is breathable. I can't understand how it is possible although I've seen Ranan and Sorgan and my friends on the *Harley* do it countless times without ill effects. For me it was unnatural. The first time I was given serious tranquilizers and yet my internal fears were so great I became violent and fought against climbing into the baths. I was told that it was too dangerous to go into the baths unconscious and that if I didn't take the baths willingly the crew would force me. Well, they had to force me. I struggled against four of them as best I could. They forced my head under the fluid and I struggled and twisted and fought for at least four minutes, refusing to take a breath. My lungs were on fire and finally I could no longer resist and I inhaled. I expected to die. I panicked and struggled and . . . suddenly I could breathe. I was so surprised that I was breathing water that I stopped struggling and never became aware of the temperature in the chamber dropping. And then I slept.

''I insisted that, among the subliminal messages sent to me while I slept to help me learn as I slept and to keep me up to date with what was happening on the ship and in the world, they include a daily session in which I was implored to speak with the elders. Something deep inside of me had told me that if I didn't attempt to talk to the elders at least every day—even if I were asleep—then the elders would leave me.

"I was in suspended animation the first time for two years. Then I was awakened and stayed awake for about six months before going back in the baths. I would like to say that the second time and the third time and the fourth time were easier than that first time, but they weren't. I fought as hard the subsequent times as I did the first time. I don't think my mind will ever be able to overcome its training to avoid breathing fluids."

He reached for another button.

After two hours of questions, Asorg announced that he would have to take a break to attend to bodily functions, a comment that drew applause and laughter from the crowd of journalists, some of whom were getting desperate for a break as well. Ranan strode to the podium.

"I will try to answer questions as well," she said. "Asorg and I had very similar experiences, although I have to admit that I had no particular trouble with the baths. If Nabyla, who was in control of the crew was willing to breathe water, then certainly I should have no fear of it. In fact, I accepted the fluids willingly. Nabyla said that I have a future in space. However, right now my future is at home with Asorg and Sorgan and my daughter-to-be."

She pulled a number from the bin and a woman from *McCall's* popped up. "Congratulations on your pregnancy, Ranan. We assume that you gave birth to Sorgan vaginally on your planet. Are you going to have your daughter removed early as is the custom on Earth?" There were gasps and grumbling from the other journalists who believed the question was unseemly, overly personal, and an attempt to point out how backward the Sorgast were hygienically.

Ranan seemed confused. She searched for assistance and a NASA aide-de-camp rushed to her side and whispered to her for a couple of minutes.

Ranan nodded and began addressing the hall again. "I have to admit that I am unfamiliar with birthing methods here. On my planet we gave birth, as all women do there, through the birth canal. I understand the concept of early removal of the baby from the womb, but I will have to discuss that procedure with the elders and study it at length before I agree to it here. I thank you for bringing that to my attention. I'm sorry I can't give you a better answer. All I can say is that I will do what is best for the health of my child, who, after all, will be the first Sorgast to be born on Earth. Ranas will be our gift to our new world.''

In all, the Sorgast answered sixty-eight questions during the four-hour press conference and managed not to dump the *Harley* into hot water. They made headlines around the world and on every newscast and computer terminal. Throngs of people greeted them at every location on the globe.

The birth of Ranas—she was removed early—was another live event when the child was ready to leave the hospital. For more than a year the Sorgast were renowned celebrities. Then they decided to settle down, and raise a family in a quiet town in Arizona. And, of course, all hell broke loose.

15

ELECTRIC CARS CLEAR THE AIR IN THE BIG APPLE

THERE ARE CERTAIN DAYS IN JANUARY IN NEW YORK CITY when you marvel at how lucky we are to live in a community where the air is crisp, the sun shines brightly, and, even though the cold stings your cheeks, the slap of Jack Frost is affirmation that despite crime, pollution, homelessness, and rudeness, life really can be good.

I hadn't felt this positive in days, maybe weeks. The air was clear. It even smelled clean. Sun rays bounced off sparkling clean building facades. The sky, where you could see it between skyscrapers, was a bright blue, almost the primary shade of blue used in preschool.

I started across the street and out of the corner of my eye I saw the giant bus bearing down on me. My last thoughts were, *Why didn't I see that bus? Why didn't I hear it? And why didn't I hear any traffic noise at all? God, I hope I'm dreaming?*

I sat up in bed shivering. It was the middle of the night. The clock read 9:30. Now I was truly confused. No light except what you'd expect from the orange streetlights filtered through the curtains, yet I knew I hadn't slept for twelve hours. It must be 9:30 A.M., but where was the light? And why was I so cold? I grabbed my robe and wrapped it around me, shuffled over to the window and looked outside. I could see nothing. Then I realized the window was covered with snow. I reached for the table to locate the cigarettes and torched one of them with the new lighter I'd purchased. The butane flame nearly singed the ceiling. I lowered the flame and inspected the damage to the cigarette. It was charred to the filter. I shrugged and began puffing on it anyway. There was a faint taste of petroleum products in the smoke. *Actually*, I thought, *it's a refreshingly different taste.*

"Smokers will rationalize anything," the masculine voice said.

I whirled around to find the Guide busily rubbing a view through one of the other windows. "It's really coming down," he said. "Reminds me of the winter of . . . oh, all the winters were the same in Mohawk country. Just like this."

"I thought you told me that you'd respect my private thoughts," I said, a bit angry.

"Sorry, force of habit."

I took another drag on the cigarette and then snuffed it out. I flicked the lighter a couple of times to make sure I wouldn't start a conflagration the next time I lit up. It seemed a bit more under control.

"It's okay," I said. "In fact, there was something I was going to ask you."

"Why didn't you hear the bus before you stepped in front of it?"

I scowled. "Yes. Was I dreaming or were we 'traveling' again?"

"You'll have to decide that yourself, Shawn. Why don't you explain what you were doing just before you were run over by the bus?"

I sat down and started thinking about that clear crisp day, and a number of questions immediately popped into my mind—especially the ones about how clear the sky was, how clean the streets, how little noise there was.

''Look at the cars, Shawn.''

I was back in the middle of the street watching the bus that had just driven right through me turn the corner and disappear. I turned my attention to the cars on the street. They hummed along peacefully. There was something different about them. I inhaled the cold air of the city and then exhaled a puff of white condensed air. I stared into the mist for a second. I quickly swiveled to watch one of the automobiles drive by. I checked the tailpipes for a sign of exhaust.

That was what was missing in the picture. In the winter in New York, mists of white, yellow, brown, and black smoke poured out of the exhausts of vehicles. But there was none of that smoke or mist in this picture. There were no tailpipes at all.

I turned to the Guide and we spoke simultaneously, I asking a question, he giving the answer: ''electric cars.''

The first practical electric cars began to make their appearance in California by the end of the twentieth century. Limited in range and battery supply, the first vehicles were only good as commuter cars. But with enormous tax credits being made available by states and cities and the federal government, the popularity of electric vehicles grew and so did the technology.

In 2009, the first electric car to travel from Los Angeles to San Francisco without needing recharging was on the road; within a couple of years the electric cars had cruising ranges of close to 1,000 miles, a fact that made their substantial extra cost worthwhile.

In 2018, the city of New York banned fuel-burning motor vehicles south of Ninety-sixth Street. Parking meters included plugs for recharging while a person shopped. The benefits of electric cars in the city included a reduction in noise pollution, a reduction in petrochemical pollution, a reduction in asthma and other lung-related illnesses.

But for a number of years, pedestrian injuries increased as people were no longer warned of an approaching vehicle by the sound of its internal combustion engine.

The major breakthrough that rid the countryside of non-electric cars was the work of General Motors and NASA in developing the direct solar car battery-recharge system. That didn't get started until around 2065, sometime following the use of satellites to beam sun energy directly from space to power stations on the Earth, Moon and Mars.

Since the late twentieth century vehicles had the power to use navigational satellites to determine exactly where they were in the world and to marry that information to CD-ROM road maps maintained in vehicle computers.

Now scientists at GM came up with an idea of having space satellites beam sunlight directly to vehicle solar cells mounted on the roofs of cars. Each car had a digital code which would be uplinked to the satellite. The satellite computer could maintain a fix on an individual car and its location (if you can use the satellite to find out where you are on the ground, the satellite in orbit around the Earth can use the same information to locate you) and could communicate with the car's computer to determine if there was a need for recharging. When such a need occurred, the satellite would locate the car, whether it was parked or on the move, get a laser fix on the solar cells, and directly feed sunlight energy to that car, recharging it on the run.

While the car's position could always be tracked, the infusion of solar energy was often hindered by buildings, parking garages, tunnels, trees, and other obstacles, making manual recharging a requirement in some situations. By 2095, virtually every vehicle on the road was electric and run by solar energy.

I stood in amazement as the cars zipped by, barely making a sound aside from tires turning on the asphalt. The sun was blocked out by a two-story tractor trailer truck, three sections long that rumbled past. The noise it made startled me, the cloud of diesel fuel choked me and attacked my nostrils, throat, and lungs. I was back in New York City 1996. As the swirling black smoke pouring out of the cab's exhaust pipe engulfed me, my awe of transportation of the future faded and the gut-eating fears of something truly gruesome replaced it. I pulled the covers on my bed over my head and huddled beneath the sheets, afraid to stay awake and confront that cloud of fumes and terrified that if I closed my eyes, I'd find out what was really going to happen in the future.

16

DOES A CENTURY GO BY WITHOUT A HOLY WAR TO THIN THE POPULATION?

I WAS BURNING UP. SWEAT POURED OFF MY BROW AS I tried to wave away the smoke that invaded my pores and made my eyes run like open faucets. I pulled off my gloves, but I was still too warm. I took off my coat and scarf. I felt better but not cool.

I wiped my eyes and saw a patch of color ahead. I stumbled toward it and realized it was a field, a meadow. It was warm outside. It was summer or late spring. I staggered toward the greenery and out of the smoke and heat. I looked behind me in time to watch the steeple crack, tip, and tumble into the roof of the church. A mountain of flame plumed upward, sending glowing tinder into the clear, sunny sky.

Instead of fighting the fire, firemen were running for cover as an angry mob attacked them and their trucks, turning the vehicles over and setting them ablaze. I heard horrible sounds, and at first I thought it was the mob. But then I realized it came from inside the church. People were being burned alive inside the building. The doors of the church were barricaded and sealed with two-by-fours nailed into the side of the structure. Men and women with rifles fired at anyone who attempted to leave the building through the windows or the roof. I watched in horror as a mother, carrying a young child was wounded as she searched for a foothold on the edge of the roof. Without a sound she tumbled head over heels to the ground, her child flung away from her toward the maiming hands and feet of the tormentors.

Where are the police? I asked myself. On the ground were the bodies of several officers. In the crowd, brandishing handguns, were other uniformed police—and they were firing at the people trapped in the church.

"The world has gone mad," I said. I sought the Guide, who I knew would be nearby. He was standing not far from my side, leaning against a tree. A tear rolled down the side of his face. "What is going on?" I recognized voices as speaking English, Americanized accents. So what was happening was occurring in the United States. I shuddered at the thought.

We were helpless apparitions as humankind tore at each other with a fury reserved only for the most devastating of conflicts—religious war. The police and fire vehicles seemed ultramodern, so I assumed the pitched mayhem I was witnessing was something that was occurring well into the future.

"About 2140," the Guide said softly.

The pitched battle in the quiet Colorado town of Evergreen was typical of the viciousness of the religious warfare that actually had its beginnings early in the twenty-first century. Even before the first trip to Alpha Centauri, a cult had developed in France and Switzerland, spreading rapidly across Europe and then America, of people who were convinced that God was an alien who came to Earth, deposited his seed among the population, and then left for other planets.

The group was generally considered kooky, and established religions persecuted them with ridicule and ostracization. The children of the God Is A Spaceman (GiSAS—Gee-sas) cult were bullied, hammered, and vilified in schools. Although their overall numbers reached several hundred thousand members worldwide, the GiSAS were considered a bizarre, doltish, wacko group. Making things worse for GiSAS was their inability to find among their members anyone who was particularly articulate and charismatic.

In 2090, all that changed. The discovery of humanoids on Alpha Centauri gave the GiSAS momentum. Scientists who were impressed by the scientific bases claimed by the cult, now came forward to say that they, too, ascribed to GiSAS philosophy, which when boiled down to its essence was just like every other religion: Do unto others as you would have them do unto you—because the powerful beings that created mankind, beings that were at least three hundred thousand years more advanced than we, were going to return and punish those being evil.

Bolstered by the knowledge that other humanoids existed, scholars began looking more closely at the GiSAS philosophy. What they found was frightening. The GiSAS believed that the original creator of mankind would return and would sanctify those who had kept the faith and were true to the Original, as the aliens were called. The GiSAS pledged that upon return of the Original, members of the faithful would root out the unfaithful and sacrifice them to the Original in a show of belief and awe and dedication to the Original's majesty.

In other words, if you weren't with us when the Original returned, you would die—badly.

The numbers in the GiSAS conventions, as they called their religious assemblies, grew exponentially in the years following the first reports of humanoids on Alpha Centauri. The number fairly exploded when the *Harley* returned with the Sorgast. There were tens of millions of GiSAS followers by 2128, when U.S. researchers finally produced a DNA report on the Sorgast.

That report found that the Sorgast DNA was closer to the DNA of human beings than any other creature on Earth—even closer than the DNA extracted from the semifossilized bone marrow of Neandertal bodies discovered in 2118.

Commentators and scientists debated for years the significance of the finding. Their deliberations were upset when, in 2130, the first transmissions from the Tau Ceti expedition found humanoids on two planets in that solar system—and again, except for minor differences in skin color and hair texture—the humanoids could go into any hair salon on Earth and could convince anyone they were human.

The Tau Ceti mission took along DNA-sequencing equipment and sent a digitized DNA code sample across airless space. The sequencing again proved that the humanoids on Tau Ceti were as human as the next person.

With the information from Tau Ceti, the scientific community determined that, indeed, all four groups of humanoids—Tau Ceti-a, Tau Ceti-b, Alpha Centauri, and Earth must have been populated by the same species. Somehow an unknown people had impregnated creatures on these planets and then had gone away, allowing these colonies to develop as the various ecologies on the planets allowed.

Remarkably, the proof that they were correct in their assumptions reduced the growth rate of the GiSAS, but not the ferocity of their members' attempts to convert the rest of the world to their cult.

One organized religion after another convened ecclesiastical missions to determine how they would answer the threat from GiSAS and the new scientific information that demonstrated that mankind is far from being alone in the Universe and may in fact belong to a band of roving rapists who defile a planet and then abandon it with their human waste in charge.

In the meantime, thousands died as the more volatile of the GiSAS groups, armed with the knowledge that they alone were right, attacked the more fundamental, i.e., smaller churches and worshipers around the country.

At first the GiSAS paraded in front of churches, demanding that the congregants reject the strict Biblical discussions of Creation, a position the evangelical movement found more and more difficult to maintain as more information about human races from other planets was disseminated. In cities in Tennessee, Arkansas, Alabama, and Iowa, those confrontations became violent.

In 2138, the first of the church burnings began. An evangelical mission was torched in the middle of the night outside of Fort Smith, Arkansas. A GiSAS convention center was blown apart in Springfield, Missouri, killing a caretaker. Another GiSAS center was burned to the ground in Alton, Illinois.

By 2139, more than five hundred churches of all denominations, including the occasional synagogue or mosque, had suffered damaging attacks and scores had been destroyed. The body count had remained low since virtually all of the attacks occurred at night.

Until the Sunday morning in June in 2140 in Evergreen. A mob of GiSAS in the community where the GiSAS numbered better than seventy percent of the population converged on the evangelical cult which had secured the lease on a former Methodist church. Most of the Methodists had either fled to other communities because of the fierceness of the local GiSAS group, or had joined up with GiSAS. The GiSAS, which had been claiming religious victory in the city, suddenly found that the closed church was reopening and the cursed, nonscientific evangelical Bible believers were moving in.

Just moments after the first prayers began, GiSAS members carrying torches overpowered police trying to separate the groups and began what became known as the Massacre at Evergreen. More than one hundred men, women, and children died in the attack, almost all of them evangelicals or police or other citizens who tried to intervene. At least four GiSAS members died, apparently crushed in the stampede to kill.

The Massacre at Evergreen was a call to arms for all sides, and blood flowed in virtually every town, city, and hamlet in the world. Entire villages were destroyed in Europe and Asia. Somehow, neither side managed to get hold of nuclear weapons, although there were several raids made on nuclear weapons facilities in the U.S., Russia, and Israel. All were repulsed. But the killings and massacres continued unabated.

For better than fifteen years conflict raged. Civilian governments attempted to staunch the blood flow by sending in army units to protect churches or separate foes. But the armies fought among themselves. GiSAS troops would not fire on their fellow believers and, instead, turned on troops who either believed in other doctrines or were following commanders' orders. The bloodshed reached all levels of leadership of the church groups, including the chieftains of the GiSAS convention, who died when their airplane exploded over the Atlantic on the way to an international peace summit.

"All wars are brutal and encourage their own atrocities, but wars over whose faith is correct tend to reach a new level of barbarism, and this war was no different in this regard. When you believe you are right and others are wrong, there is no limit to the horror you can produce on your enemy. Rape, torture, murder in an extreme and foul manner occurred without warning and without remorse," the Guide told me, sorrow hanging from his lips.

In 2158, a papal bull determined that there was no conflict between the teachings of Jesus Christ and the fact that human beings existed on planets outside the Earth. The Pope chastised those who believed that the Almighty was not powerful enough to have created not only human beings on Earth but on hundreds of other planets as well.

But, the pontiff decreed, there is no reason to believe that Jesus as the Son of God was any less a deity Himself simply because there were humans on other planets. "Who," the Pope asked rhetorically, "created the aliens that gave us human characteristics? Were not those aliens also the creation of God? Would they also not be children of the Son of God?" The Pope required a reaffirmation of faith in the teachings of Jesus and demanded an end to worldwide bloodshed. "We are simply arguing over the same point and we are forgetting the most important point: We are all brothers, no matter the color of our skin, the way we pray, or the planet on which we were born."

Leaders of other religions adopted similar messages. The theme of brotherhood washed over the land and cleansed it of the blood spilled in religious warfare. Historians would declare the wars over in 2166, and would attribute two hundred and twelve million deaths around the world to the GiSAS Wars.

"How could something like that happen—especially one hundred and fifty years in the future?" I asked the Guide, as we stared at the dying embers of the church in Evergreen. "Haven't we learned anything?"

The Guide just arched his eyebrows and grimaced.

"For hundreds of years mankind has worried about how it was going to feed itself as the population of the society continued to grow. And every generation figures out a way to keep population in line, either through massive war or massive disease. The twenty-second century residents of the planet are no different than any other generation, to be dogged by war which will claim the best and the brightest and prevent mankind from reaching to the stars which are its destiny."

Don't want my daughter dating someone with green skin

I HAD JUST STARTED DINNER—REMOVING THE FOIL WRAP from the potpie and setting the timer on the microwave— when I felt a presence behind me. Despite three years of being regularly surprised by the appearance of the Guide, I still maintained a New York City-woman's knowledge that sooner or later you would have to confront an intruder in your home or an accoster on the street. I casually let my hand locate the butcher knife on the sink countertop, grasped the haft, and whirled to confront—nothing.

I searched the corners and crevices of the kitchen, and I silently crept into the living room of the apartment. And there was the Guide, sitting in my favorite chair, one hand petting my cat and the other trying to locate something on a map in the massive National Geographic Atlas.

He glanced at me and went back to the map. "Don't put it down," he said. "Maybe if it ever stops snowing we can go hunting for some food. There won't be any in the markets."

It had been snowing in New York for a week, and the mayor had ordered all nonessential vehicles off the streets, so naturally everyone got in their cars and tried to drive around, creating gridlock. The airports were closed; not even trains were running. New Yorkers are quick to complain about almost anything that makes life in the Big Apple miserable, and there is plenty to complain about, and one of the favorites is ConEdison, the power company. Well, if nothing else was working in the city, the power stayed on, so homes were comfortable. Food, on the other hand, was hard to find. The potpie had been hiding in the back of my freezer for so long I refused to check the label to see when I had purchased it. It was at least a year old, probably a lot older, but it represented one of the few sources of calories left in the refrigerator.

"Had a rough night?" he asked softly.

I nodded.

"Want to talk about it?"

"It was my grandfather. I dreamed about him again. He was talking to me, trying to soothe me. I was upset again— about meeting you. He was trying to let me know everything was all right. That you were to be trusted. That I should trust my best instincts."

"Were you talking to him?"

"No . . . yes. I guess I was. But it was in a dream. You do a lot of crazy things when you are dreaming. Like talking to dead people who show up in the dreams."

"And when you are awake, or think you are awake, you talk to Mohawks who have been dead for centuries. Right?"

I laughed. "Well, you are just confirmation that I'm really going out of my mind."

"Anybody else you know talk to the dead?"

"I've got a lot of psychic friends who claim to converse with those in the afterlife, although they maintain that those discussions occur while they are conscious or in some kind of altered consciousness."

"Like they are dreaming?"

"Yes, I suppose so. But why are we discussing this? And what are you looking at?"

I realized I was slashing air with the butcher knife and
nearly stabbed myself in the side. I put down the knife and
peered over the Guide's shoulder. He was checking a map
of the Southwest, Arizona, Phoenix . . . no north of Phoenix . . .

The red stones, carved by centuries of winds and waters
guard the entrance to Sedona, one of the centers of mystical
life in the United States. I'd never traveled to the strange
city north of Phoenix, but dozens of my psychic friends
went there to be ''recharged.''

The streets of Sedona were quieter than usual, and I
quickly noted that was due to the purring electric cars that
cruised past one shop after another advocating some New
Age device or philosophy. The Guide was alongside, pointing out the store offering crystals and guides to crystal therapy; the pyramid purveyors were next door, and so was a
bookstore which displayed not the latest novels but the new
book by Asorg Sorgast, *You Can Meet Your Elders, Too.*

''They had to display it big,'' the Guide said. ''Local
author.''

After a successful world tour and the successful birth of
Ranas, the Sorgast decided to settle in Sedona, Arizona, a
place, they were told, having great harmony in the world.
The U.S. Congress had unanimously granted the Sorgast
citizenship, especially after Ranas was born in the state-of-
the-art birthing complex at Montefiore Hospital in the
Bronx. That automatically gave her citizenship, and politicians decided to ride the tide of public adoration for the
Sorgast by awarding the rights of the daughter to her parents and brother.

Officials from every state lobbied to have the Sorgast put
down roots there, but federal authorities were pleased with
the selection of Sedona, a community far from the persis-
tent eyes of national media, in an area of great tolerance
for different people, ideologies, and eccentricities. Just
walking down the streets of Sedona you would likely see
people dressed as Native Americans; women wearing saris;
men in spacesuits to ward off pollutants; men wearing tur-
bans; a flower child or two who were throwbacks to the
1960s.

The Guide and I found a bench and watched as the parade of strange human-life forms went by. The Guide pointed to an ice-cream parlor, advertising the tastiest pure ice cream with no preservatives, no sugar, no fats, no lactates, no calories. "What is it made of?" I asked. "Your imagination?"

"Close enough," he said. He nudged me and nodded to his left. Walking down the street was a group of five teenagers who were still keeping Levi's in business even in the year 2129. The three girls were giggling; the two boys accompanying them seemed totally at a loss about what the joke was. One of the boys stared in our direction, a puzzled look on his face. Then he turned his attention to the crowd. They all seemed normal enough, except for the one who looked over at us. His face was green.

"He could see us," I gasped.

"Yes," said the Guide.

We looked at each other. I was still dressed in my robe and slippers that resembled squirrels; he was in his favorite warrior outfit. I laughed. We fit in well for an afternoon in Sedona.

"So," I said, "that must have been Sorgan. He's growing up." Sorgan was about five-foot-nine, which made him slightly taller than his father. He was broad-shouldered and didn't look ill fed. Psychically something bothered me, however. "He's having a tough time here, isn't he?" I asked.

"They all are."

The citizens of Sedona were ecstatic when they found out in 2128 that the Sorgast had decided to settle in their community. There were parades and welcoming parties and invitations to all of the local, regional, and some national events in Sedona. The Sorgast were the toast of the town.

All the friendship toward them, however, began to change when Sorgan, chronologically twenty-two Earth years old, but physically only about eleven, was entered into junior high school. He was at once a likable curiosity and a threat to the ordered structure of public-school life.

The girls flocked to him, seeking to have some of his fame rub off on them; some of the boys he befriended were cocky with achievement; those Sorgan chose not to be close to became enemies. He was invited to stay overnight at friends' homes and spent hours on the visiphone talking to a cadre of girls.

The resentments built up quickly. While they were based in the fact that Sorgan was more popular owing to his vastly different experiences, it was easier to poke fun at his skin color than admit jealousy. Sorgan wasn't a brute, although he had superior strength, but he wasn't a diplomat, either. There were fights. He usually won, unless there were two or three or four against him. These he usually lost, and came home with bruises and more than one bloody nose.

He was particularly sensitive about his skin color, about which he could do nothing and which made him easily noticeable in a crowd. Cries of "Lizard boy" and "Jolly Green Giant" trailed after him in the school corridors and on the streets. His first year in school was chaotic and miserable.

He wanted to leave and live somewhere else, but Asorg counseled him otherwise. "You are always going to have green skin, and there are only going to be Sorgast with green skin. You can't run away from your skin. Those who have tried it are scorned by all sides. You have to live with who you are. You are skilled, you are athletic, you are intelligent, and you—at least you'd better try—are a representative and example of your race and your people here on Earth and back on Alpha Centauri. Learn to live with it. You will be far happier if you can do that. Remember that those who mock you show themselves up for what they are—ignorant bigots."

What Asorg didn't tell him was that he and Ranan were extremely happy in Sedona, where they were accepted with open arms into the community. As a couple devoted to each other and their family, they were no sexual threat to anyone's spouse or sweetheart. Their naïveté in social situations enchanted their social circle; their willingness to endorse stores and products without demands made them welcome in stores and shops.

Even so a cloud hung over their heads as the religious war between the established churches and the GiSAS heated. The GiSAS cited the Sorgast as one of the precepts of their faith—despite the fact that the Sorgast joined no religious organization, preferring their own faith, the communion with the elders. It was the Sorgast strength of faith in their own religious rites that developed a following and kept the Sorgast at arm's length from the chaos the religious wars had on the rest of the world.

The combination of the presence of the Sorgast in Sedona and the fact that so many forms of worship existed in the community kept the scourge of the religious wars from creating much of an impact on the city. The closest Sedona came to violence over the religious issue erupted at a town meeting to discuss religious tolerance when a group of atheists demanded that they be included in the forum as well as everyone else. Without hesitation they were seated and remained silent throughout the session.

At this session, Asorg was again asked to discuss his relationship with the elders. It was a constant surprise to Asorg that Earth people were so interested in the contacts with the elders, and it mystified him why Earth people didn't have the ability to contact their own elders.

"We believe that life is never-ending. The elders we talk to every day, sometimes several times a day, are our parents, our friends, our leaders who have left the tactile world and have entered the ethereal world. You say that these people have died. We say they have passed to the other form, a higher form.

"What you refer to as ghosts, apparitions, spirits, and Guardian Angels are not figments of the imagination but are real and are ever-present," Asorg explained. He explained it so often, that he was encouraged to write about it. His book sold well in Sedona, although not as well elsewhere. Even so, royalties kept coming in.

His funds were managed by a special government office, created by the special legislation that gave him citizenship, that made sure he lived comfortably and paid his taxes. Congress didn't want ever to have the embarrassment of the first visitor from another planet being evicted by some marshal for failure to pay taxes.

In his book, Asorg claimed that everyone had the ability to see elders, except that by the time most people lost an important person in their life to death, those persons were already at an age when the ability to see elders had been lost. Asorg wrote that the elders had told him that to commune with those on the elders' side of reality required daily attention to communication. That's why, when Sorgan was only a baby, he was instructed in how to conduct séances with his parents. The ability wasn't automatic, the elders told Asorg, it was something that had to be mastered at an early age and performed regularly. "Use it or lose it," they said.

Asorg suggested that failure to use it denied Earthlings the power to visit their elders. He described his rituals and how they worked, holding out hope that constant attempts might revive the ember of contact in each person's brain. Tens of thousands who read his books tried his methods; very few reported any success, and those that did report success were later revealed to be suffering from long-term psychosis.

The ability to commune with elders remained, for decades, the true difference between Sorgast and Earthmen.

The knife clattered to the floor. I had forgotten it was there and knocked it to the ground. It missed my foot by inches.

"Planning surgery?" the Guide asked.

I picked up the potential amputee maker and took it into the kitchen. Then I returned. Queenie, the sixteen pounds of white fluff, had flattened herself into the easy chair, giving me one of those this-is-my-place-Buster looks. I decided against sitting down and wandered over to the window and watched the snow drift.

"I see the dead and it usually takes some sort of trance-like trigger for me. A dream, a flicker of light, someone's soothing voice. Maybe I can see elders, too?" I suggested to the Guide.

"You've been using your ability for years. Perhaps not as powerfully as the Sorgast, but enough to make it possible for you to see me, talk to me, and hear what I have to say—and then recall it. The skills you have are the same those aliens have and that's because you are both human beings with similar genetic structures and abilities.

"However, you are one of a very small number of people who have maintained those abilities since childhood, even against the wishes of those closest to you. Very few people today have done that. That's why you have psychic powers that others do not."

"Are you saying that I'm psychic because I can speak to my 'elders'?"

"I'm sure that's part of it. Most likely there are other factors as well."

"What other factors?"

"I don't know. Genes, perhaps."

"Psychic genes? People have psychic genes? Are you kidding me?"

18

THE TAU CETI VISIT DELAYED BY CHAOS AND WAR

THE TAU CETI HAD BEEN STUDIED FOR NEARLY A GEN-
eration while they were parked on the Moon during the
religious wars.

The mission to their planets had been extraordinary in
that the Earthmen were able to deal with a well-developed
society on each of the two planets.

The Alphas were closer to their sun, but lived on a larger
planet than the Betas, whose world was less than half the
size of the Alphas'. Both worlds had similar climates and
atmospheres, which accounted for their development being
similar.

The Alphas were roughly equivalent to the Middle Eastern societies in pre-Christian times. The people lived in
small cities and towns and were familiar with agriculture;
understood the dynamics of seasons, and had studied astronomy with more or less decent results in predicting occurrences such as eclipses and tides. As with their kindred
souls on the nearby third planet, the Alphas had experienced the scourge of war as factions struggled over land

distribution. The winners lived in cities near water sources; the losers lived in mountains and forests and engaged in guerrilla warfare, sneak attacks, and survived on hunting forest game.

Domesticated animals existed on both planets, although the Alphas were beset by periodic attacks by swarms of half-insect, half-mammalian creatures which made suicide raids on the villages standing between the creatures and potable water. The creatures were not only savagely destroyed by the Alphas during these raids, but also became delicacies during victory feasts.

The Betas were marginally more advanced, having evidence of well-developed transportation between cities and villages. The Earth visitors saw roads and crude ships that transported goods across water. Intercity trade flourished. Astronomy was at the same level as the Alphas' science. Both the Alphas and Betas had a sense of history and an appreciation of art and knowledge of their planet. They were well aware of the planets in their solar system, and even though the two inhabited planets were only about twenty-five million miles apart, neither conceived that the other could be inhabited by such similar creatures.

In fact, there were few if any differences between the inhabitants. It was now obvious that the Tau Ceti forebears were the same, and they were the same as those on Alpha Centauri and Earth.

When the crew of the mission made themselves known to the people on the planet, they were met with little hostility. Certain religious factions on the planet had claimed there would be a visit from outside their world, so on Alpha, at least, the welcome was cordial. However, the Alpha astronomers were skeptical that the men who commanded these technological marvels that had landed among the villages could have possibly come from such a woeful-looking star as Sol. They pointed to all the brilliant stars in their heavens and were disappointed to find that Earthmen came from such an insignificant-looking one.

There were many offers to join the mission for its long trip back to Earth for study. The community's chiefs, selected popularly if not elected democratically, considered

the impact of sending people to Earth—never to return for
the lifetimes of those there now. They determined that a
historian, his daughter and son-in-law and their son, and a
military officer and his spouse would offer the best from
their world for further study on Earth.

The Betas suggested an elderly historian and his spouse
as well as a trader, his spouse and two children, and six
children ranging in age from eight to sixteen from an or-
phanage. The children were offered a chance to start a new
life on Earth. The Beta society was one in which a child's
future depended on his parents' background and business.
Businesses and lands and ships were handed down from
father to son. The patriarchal society also had little use for
female children aside from the production of additional
children. The orphans had little chance of becoming self-
sufficient in the Beta society. They understood and needed
little convincing to make the trip to Earth.

It was relatively easy to develop a dictionary of the Tau
Ceti languages, and soon everyone was speaking either Alpha, Beta, or English interchangeably. None of the aliens,
however, took to the suspended-animation baths without a
serious struggle. The mission directors allowed the Tau Cetians to avoid their first baths until they could see a few
crewmen inhale the fluids, be numbed into suspended animation, and then be revived without apparent ill effects.

It gave the mission an extra year to understand the Tau
Cetians and for the Tau Cetians to get used to being called
Tau Cetians or Alphas or Betas. As with the Alpha Cen-
turions, each group identified his home as "Earth" and his
sun as "the Sun" in the appropriate language.

The crew raced along to Earth, unaware that their an-
nouncements had helped pour kerosene on the smoldering
GiSAS religious conflagration on Earth. When they arrived
in the solar system in 2145 and realized that Earth was in
chaos, the Tau Cetians were taken to the Moon, where a
domed home was created for them and where they were to
sit out the disaster on Earth.

The Moon-based Tau Cetians were an unhappy bunch
when they finally were able to touch down on the planet
they had heard so much about for so long a time. But when

they were shown the technological wonders of their new home, their peevishness melted, and they embraced the land.

To lessen possible discrimination like that the Sorgast had encountered, the Tau Cetians, originally numbering eighteen people, now having grown to thirty, were kept in a separate community, close to the aloof Hutterite sects of Washington state. The Hutterites had managed to remain out of the religious war zones, and their isolationist policies protected them against contagious disease plagues that engulfed the world as well.

The braver of the Tau Cetians moved out of the colony within a few years and took to the lure of cities such as Los Angeles and New York, where their slightly orange skin and hair tint seemed little strange to the denizens of the twenty-million-citizen metropolis.

The first DNA studies of the Tau Cetians showed that there was unequivocal support that they were human. Already the Sorgast children had married Earthlings and had produced nothing but perfect children—although not without controversy.

Sorgan withstood slings and arrows of adolescence and went on to UCLA to study communication arts, eventually becoming a film student, which led him to be wooed by the avant garde film crowd in Hollywood. This, in turn, led to his being introduced to the stunning daughter of one of the nation's favorite television and movie stars.

Before you could say, "It's a wrap, let's start the sequel," Sorgan was walking down the aisle. The ceremony was literally a cast-of-thousands ceremony that was broadcast live on eleven all-news cable channels. The wedding was protested by sheet-covered groups (they said they were not Ku Klux Klan, but sympathized with the principles of the KKK) who declared that it was against God's law for green-skinned aliens to have intercourse with Caucasian women.

The protesters, watched with disgust by thousands of movie fans who weren't invited to the wedding, were pelted with wedding cake by departing wedding guests. A picture taken of a mongrel dog licking icing off the hood of a slumped-over protester won the Pulitzer prize for photography for 2147.

Sorgan's sister Ranas married four years later in a quiet ceremony in Tahiti to the son of a Tibetan crystal salesman. The marriage barely made the Internet gossip columns.

When the world finally regained its sanity, and the religious chasm over who were the true believers in the Children of the Aliens was patched if not healed, researchers started tracking down the next great mystery of the Sorgast and the Tau Cetians—the secrets of the elders.

In interviews with Tau Cetians, it was determined that an ability to speak to the departed existed among them. But of the eighteen that came ten-plus light-years, only two of them—an orphaned brother and sister—claimed the ability to communicate with their parents, grandparents, and others. Their fellow Tau Cetians considered them strange, but it was well-known on each of the Tau Ceti planets that such communication occurred, although it was not common practice.

Scientists descended upon the two children, now grown adults who had married other Tau Cetians, and their offspring to study their contacts with elders. The orphans had insisted that they would raise their children with elders, and their spouses were in agreement.

By 2176, the research teams had found that the two Tau Ceti families engaged in regular discussions with elders. The researchers tracked down Sorgan and Ranas and found that they were engaged in the same ceremonies with their mixed Centauri-Earth children. Interestingly, Sorgan's spouse—the actor's daughter—claimed that she was able to talk to her grandfather and several of her friends who had died when their drug-dazed pilot mistook twelve-lane Interstate 10 for the main runway at Los Angeles International Airport and failed to glide the plane under a highway overpass.

In a stunning scientific paper in 2179, scientists said that they had isolated a special gene from the blood of the Tau Cetians, the Sorgast, and the Centauri-Earth offspring that they believed triggered the production of an enzyme which triggered a genetic switch allowing the brain to pierce the boundary between the tactile world and the other dimension. Higher levels of this enzyme were also detected in Sorgan's spouse.

Newspapers went tabloid in screaming: "Pathway to the dead discovered," "Call to the dead just a gene away," and the like. Overnight, colleges established courses on how the discovery would change the world; myriad books popped up on the subject of communication with the dead; sermonizers exploited the message of everlasting life; ghostbusting agencies that had been mocked ran "I told you so" advertisements; Asorg Sorgast's books were dusted off and reprinted by his publisher, and he was sent out on the lecture circuit; ethicists, lawyers, and politicians debated the necessity of changing statutes to prevent people from committing suicide knowing they could take life with them and at least allow their friends and offspring the fruits of their deeds. It was a time of wonder.

But like all times of wonder, the stench of reality soon made people gag. While science had discovered the mechanisms which allowed Asorg, Sorgan, the Tau Cetians, and a handful of psychics to communicate beyond the pale, finding a way to trigger the response among the average person who hadn't practiced communicating over the years was elusive.

But when science finds that the public wants, demands, and insists on a solution—and the public is willing to spend the nation's treasury on such a development, almost anything can be accomplished.

The GiSAS society offered a staggering billion-dollar reward to the first scientist who could develop a way to trigger the cascade of events that opened the door to the elders. It was matched by Bristol-Myers Squibb Merck Bayer, the interplanetary pharmaceutical giant which also pledged $3 billion in grants to scientists in the field. It still took until 2196 before the compound was synthesized and another ten years before its toxicity and dosage were determined.

In 2206, the compound was eagerly snatched up by millions of people, who were stunned to find that while the drug worked, they could not contact lost parents and friends. Asorg explained, "You must make contact with your elders shortly after they cross over. If they cannot reach you and you cannot reach them, they become detached and move away. They are unrecoverable. That's why we begin the séances at birth. We have to keep those genes viable so that when a loss occurs that loss can be captured and kept close for all time. You can't achieve it with drugs. It has to come from the heart, from faith, and for all time.''

Actually Asorg was right and wrong, later research proved. If you start when you are young you will maintain the power to communicate with those on the other side for a lifetime. For those who have lost the power, the compound would activate the atrophied system, allowing for communications with friends, relatives, children, spouses who might pass to the other side in the future, proving again that nothing is as good as it seems it could be nor is anything as bad either.

HOW A PEST TURNED
LAKE ERIE'S FISH EDIBLE

"WHAT YOU'VE SAID SO FAR IS REALLY FASCINATING. BUT I've got to tell you there are a few details I'm having trouble with."

One of the downsides of telling psychic stories to journalists is that they always have a couple of extra questions. My friend and confidant, Ed Susman, was one of those people. He reminded me of Columbo, the detective that Peter Falk made famous on television. Columbo always had one more question to ask a suspect until the suspect's story collapsed like a house of cards.

"So what's your question this time?" I asked, trying to keep my tone a shade toward sarcasm and not toward frustration.

"What you seem to be telling me is that we all have this power to see people who affected our lives after they died. The problem is that if that power is not activated and utilized virtually from birth, we lose the ability to use it and lose that power forever."

"That . . ."

"Wait, let me complete my thought, here. And in addition to losing the power to seek these people who have died and live in this netherworld or spiritworld, those in that other place lose the power to contact us. Is that the idea?"

"That's how I understand it. That's what I feel the Guide has told me."

"Okay, then," he said in his best attempt to imitate Jim Carrey, "the Guide has been dead a few centuries. You never knew him when he was alive because you haven't yet lived half a century. How come you can talk to the Guide?"

"I asked him that."

"And . . . ?"

"He explained that there are a limited number of 'Guides' like himself that can locate people who seek the spirit world and I'm apparently one of them."

"That's so . . ."

"Simple? Aren't you the one who told me that the simplest answer is usually the most likely answer?"

"Yeah, except it doesn't usually work for Los Angeles juries."

Ed had been upset by the result in the O.J. Simpson trial for months. He was convinced the evidence would convict Simpson no matter who was on the jury. I had told him Simpson would walk. He said he could accept that the jury found him not guilty, but he'd never accept that he was innocent.

"Any other questions?" I parried.

"No, not right now. But there was something you mentioned about fishing in Lake Erie, or was it Lake Ontario."

"Oh yes, but it wasn't me that said that. It was the Guide."

"Shawn, it had to be you. I don't speak to the Guide. I only speak to you. Remember, I'm not yet ready to believe that this Guide exists."

"When you talk to me, and when I go into a trance, you aren't talking to me. You are actually talking to the Guide, but you are talking to him through me. Do you understand?"

"The concept I can accept. It's just really, really hard

for me to believe that I'm talking to someone who's been dead since before Hiawatha was born and now can take you on a travelogue to the future.''

"Well, all I can say is that if you want to know about fishing in Lake Erie and Lake Ontario, you are going to have to get that information from the Guide.''

Dead air.

"No sense in fighting this, but this had better be an interesting story because it's going to be a long time before someone takes a fish out of those lakes, eats it, and then doesn't test positive for mercury poisoning.''

I stretched out in the easy chair, using both hands to lift the white ball of fur that was Queenie. The cat opened one of her eyes, then closed it again and began her light purring. She trusted me so well that she was certain I would replace her in my lap, which is exactly what I did.

"I'm ready," I told him, resting the phone on my shoulder. He began speaking slowly and quietly, asking me routine questions about where I was and what I was seeing and . . .

In fact, it took a long time for the two of the most polluted of the Great Lakes to be put back in shape again—and it turned out to be a rogue mollusk that was responsible.

In the early 1980s, scientists began to notice that a sea creature, the zebra mussel, had appeared in the colder waters of North America. The mussel was a native of the Far East and its presence disturbed researchers and environmentalists. In areas where humans thrived, so did the mussel. It attached itself to the hulls of ships; it grouped in monstrous colonies on piers; it was especially interested in the intake and outlet pipes of sewer and water drainage systems. It was a pest, and no one had much success in eradicating it.

The mussel was believed to have somehow survived a trip through the St. Lawrence Seaway System from the Far East, and scientists tracked its spread with concern and fear. It was soon found throughout the Great Lakes. The zebra mussels drifted with the currents or against them and established colonies up the Genesee River, which flows through Rochester, New York, and threatened the pristine Finger Lakes. The mussel prowled the Chicago River and made its way into the Mississippi River system. It roamed up the Ohio River past Pittsburgh, to the Allegheny and Monongahela Rivers and into lakes and streams in Pennsylvania, Ohio, and West Virginia.

And it created havoc along the way. Piers collapsed when tons of zebra mussel colonies attached themselves to pilings. Boaters spent millions of dollars keeping their boats clean, then had to spend tens of thousands more getting their boats sterilized before they could enter zebra mussel-free waters of the deep cold lakes of upstate New York. Thousands of dollars were spent monitoring the lakes for the arrival of the zebra mussels, but nothing seemed to be able to stop the spread of the creatures.

Taxpayers were spending millions to keep water-purifying systems clear of the mussels, but nothing seemed to work. In 2017, the mussels reached New Orleans, and before city politicians could decide which crony deserved the contract for keeping the mussels out of the pipes, the city's sewage plant stopped functioning, backing up sewage throughout the Big Easy. Wags said it was months before anyone thought the smell was unusual, but the immediate crisis was resolved within a week.

Appealing to Congress, Louisiana and other affected states finally were able to get some serious money spent to wipe out the pest. The main problem in trying to get rid of the zebra mussel was that you didn't dare poison the creature for fear of killing everything else in the waterways.

Scientists again turned to genetic engineering. One plan of action was to find female mussels and put them through a series of genetic hoops to create a species that was more fertile than the present species but would only produce female mussels, a procedure used in game fisheries to produce huge prize-winning fish—females are usually bigger fish than males.

The procedures worked, but when the female-only mussels were released, the problem worsened. The females attracted the male mussels because of their size and the females produced and produced and produced. So intent were the developers in coming up with female mussels that someone forgot to check the local dairy farms. They would have noticed that for every fifty cows there was only one bull. There were so many male zebra mussels available in all the waterways, that the experiment only succeeded in providing additional millions of larger zebra mussels—mussels that somehow had found their way all the way up the Mississippi River to the Missouri and even into the Yellowstone River in Montana.

In 2019, the West Coast began demanding more action be spent to stop the mussel because it had been found in the Colorado River—the river of life to Southern California. If the zebra mussel fouled the inlet pipes, Los Angeles would die of thirst—quickly.

In 2022, scientists announced that they had finally developed a weapon to fight the zebra mussel. A genetically altered underwater worm was created to seek out only zebra mussels. The worm's DNA is so constructed that when it encounters a zebra mussel, the worm secretes a fluid that enters the mussel, invades it, attaches to the mussel's DNA, and destroys it. The government ordered tons of the worms developed, but before they decided to use it a social scientist in Ontario discovered that children who were being fed fish that their lower socioeconomic status parents have caught in Lake Erie to supplement the family's protein intake were nòt suffering from metal poisoning.

Instead of finding high levels of lead, mercury, cadmium, and other metals known to be lurking in Lake Erie, the researcher found nothing but healthful benefits of the fish. The report put on hold the government's decision to dump a ton of the anti–zebra mussel worm into the lake. An aquaculture team began studying the lake and found that not only were the fish safe to eat, but there were fish thriving in the lake that hadn't been seen there for half a century.

When they analyzed the reason, they found that somehow the zebra mussels were devouring the algae in the lakes, making them clearer and cleaner and making healthier plants and fish thrive. Incredibly, not only was the lake almost returned to a pristine condition, but the fish that had returned were avid fans of the zebra mussel—as their diet of choice.

The attack on the zebra mussel was put on hold, and the stores of the worms were destroyed in 2032. In the interim, scientists used gene therapy to devise a substance that the zebra mussel hates and that substance, which is toxic to nothing else, was painted on boats, pilings, and water pipes, ending the zebra mussel threat to man-made objects. Several states will eventually name the zebra mussel, now a hero in the war against pollution, as their State Mollusk.

20

HIGH WATER AND NEW PLAGUES SWAMP THE EARTH

EVEN BEFORE I COULD ADJUST MY EYES AND GET MY bearings, I knew we were in a hospital. The smell of disinfectant just wasn't enough to wash away the lingering substrate of illness, decay, dying tissue, and death. But in this hospital, the disinfectant was the substrate, the corridors reeked with the loathsome odors that made one's stomach turn.

From room after room came moans and cries and long-winded incoherent diatribes punctuated by coughs, wheezes, gurgles, and intermittent retching sounds. Small knots of doctors, nurses, and red-eyed men and women huddled outside the doors. From their expressions, the news about someone's loved one wasn't pleasant.

The hospital seemed to be a modern facility; the voices spoke English; there was no indication that this was any facility other than a state-of-the-art facility in the world's most medically advanced society. Yet death surrounded us.

"AIDS?" I asked the Guide.

He shook his head. "Dengue hemorrhagic fever."

"A deadly reaction to overuse of Bengay ointment by overzealous, overage, and out-of-shape would-be athletes?" I tried.

He almost smiled.

Actually some synapse in my brain did deliver recognition of dengue. Maybe it was something Dan Rather had said. I equated it with a tropical disease. But I sensed I was out of place for the tropics. I looked out the window of the hospital to the magnificent view of the city skyline in the distance. The vista was dominated by a huge arch—St. Louis, the Gateway Arch.

The trees were green. Men and women were dressed in short sleeves, walking shorts, and short skirts. I hunted for clues of the time and place, and spotted a calendar at the nurses' station—February, 2116.

Nothing made sense. St. Louis? February? People walking in shorts? Tropical fever patients filling up hospital beds?

I put on my best puzzled face and turned to the Guide.

"Global warming."

"Huh?"

Scientists spent decades warning the world that unless humankind changed its evil ways of befouling its own planet, there would be an irreversible change in the climate of the Earth. The most radical of the doomsayers predicted the most dire of consequences: Gases from fossil fuel-burning heating plants would create so much pollution that it would trigger a greenhouse effect.

The pollution would blanket the Earth, destroying the ozone layers and letting deadly ultraviolet rays through the misty blanket, causing everyone on Earth to come down with melanoma. The sun's rays would heat up the planet, and the blanket of smog would prevent that heat from being released into space. Temperatures would rise on Earth, destroying plants and animals, then mankind itself. The heating would continue until the planet became so hot that the oceans boiled and killed what was left of underwater life. Then, with the planet bare and lifeless, the now barren planet would continue to heat until even the atmosphere boiled away, making the Earth as uninhabitable as Mercury.

The models promulgated by the extremists saw this action taking as little as a couple of generations before total destruction of the planet was at hand.

"Actually," said the Guide, "it took a couple of generations before scientists finally agreed that there was a statistically significant change in climate at all. And yes, indeed, they found, the Earth was getting warmer. If ever so slowly."

By the end of the twentieth century, scientists found about a one-to-two degree change in mean temperatures. The planet was certainly getting warmer, even though that didn't prevent winters of continuing blizzards. By the year 2100, however, the global warming had increased. Scientists again disseminated dire warnings, but when you asked how much warmer it was than in 2001, the answer was, "A little more than two degrees Fahrenheit."

The pronouncement was greeted with a yawn among most of the seven billion people on Earth. Two hundred years of debate and warnings and it was likely only to get down to six degrees during January in Green Bay, instead of three degrees.

There were some areas where there was a greater concern over the effects of global warming. The minuscule rise of two degrees in temperature in turn meant that a bit of the polar ice caps and certain high-mountain glaciers had melted, and those caps had shrunk in size. It was enough of a melt to raise the level of the world's oceans about two feet.

Again, that statistic drew scant attention in Denver. In Palm Beach, however, it was a local catastrophe. After spending hundreds of millions of dollars over the past century to maintain a beach in Palm Beach, the most affluent community (per capita) in the United States finally gave up.

The beach in Palm Beach had disappeared in the 1980s, a result of the combination of rising oceans and the constant pounding of the Atlantic Ocean. The beach disappeared right up to the seawall, and the town took some devastating hits from glancing hurricanes, which demolished the decorative wall, turned beachfront cottages into flotsam, undermined oceanfront roads, water, and sewer systems, and even threatened multimillion-dollar homes, condominiums, and historic landmarks.

Each time the beach would wash away, the town would dig into its incredibly deep pockets and come up with funds to recreate the beach, sometimes building formations seventy-five yards into the ocean, then spending a year filling them with sand—all the time keeping the residents off the beach until the project was completed. The beach was rebuilt in 1995, then again in 2008, and a third time in 2022. That third attempt was to be the mother of all beaches, extending the beach four hundred feet from shore for one mile. It cost the town's taxpayers close to a billion dollars, but as one councilman said, "Palm Beach without a beach is not Palm Beach."

The forces of nature and the detriment of mankind, however, combined to erode the mother of all beaches in record time. In 2024, the town closed the entrances to the ocean permanently and spent several hundred million dollars reinforcing the seawall. Instead of a beach, Palm Beach constructed at twenty-foot-wide, half-mile-long concrete barrier to hold back the sea.

In 2083, a not particularly violent hurricane churned off Palm Beach for three days, soaking the area with thirty-six inches of rain and hurling tides and waves up to fifteen feet high against the concrete barricade. The barricade lost. Again the town retreated, this time turning the roadway along the beach in to a forty-foot-wide pillar of concrete. People still came to Palm Beach to sunbathe, but now they were relaxing on concrete instead of sand. Condominium owners were treated to a terrifying view of the ocean lapping at the sides of their building at every solstice tide.

That only lasted for twenty-five years. In 2108, the town council decided that the homes and condominiums were not long suitable for habitation. People living in those homes were allowed to stay, but repairs and reconstruction were not permitted. The once stately and costly residences took on the air of a ghost town. One by one, as residents died or finally decided to leave, the homes were demolished. An elevated roadway was built over the sites of the razed homes in 2133. Yet the water continued to damage the city.

The town spent over ten billion dollars trying to defeat nature, when it should have realized a lot sooner that the ocean was a lot more powerful than concrete. All they had to do was to look at the city of Galveston.

In 1900, Galveston was destroyed by a hurricane in the worst natural disaster in the history of the United States. More than six thousand people died as the storm wiped out nearly every home and business on the island off the Texas Gulf Coast.

Gritty Galveston refused to die. The city rebuilt and constructed a massive seawall designed to protect the downtown area of the city for all time. In fact, the seawall worked well. Numerous hurricanes battered the Texas Gulf Coast throughout the twentieth and twenty-first centuries without breaching the wall. But the increase of two feet in the level of the oceans was the downfall of the Galveston seawall. By 2089, the swells caused by passing pleasure craft were sufficient—at high tide—to splash water over the seawalls. When tides were abnormally high, the Gulf's water poured over the wall as if it weren't there. The receding water undermined the wall from the land side, and great chunks of concrete began to melt into the sea.

Hurricanes, even mild ones, sent wave after wave of water over the wall, drowning the city. The unprotected island south of the city disappeared, washed away with each tide and storm. It became apparent that if there was a major hurricane, the disaster of 1900 would be repeated. Even late in the twenty-first century, Galveston hadn't forgotten the bitter lessons of that disaster. On December 31, 2099, the city council of Galveston closed down the city, deeding all city-owned property, including virtually all homes and businesses that had been abandoned during the past twenty years, to the state of Texas. A line of a dozen buses were the last to cross the Interstate 45 bridge to the Texas mainland, and the history of Galveston sank with the next morning's high tide.

Remarkably, the economic and personal disasters that beset Palm Beach, Galveston, and hundreds of other resorts along the Atlantic and Pacific coasts, occurred without serious loss of life. Elsewhere in the world, the story was far different.

Atolls throughout the South Pacific and Indian Oceans would note with alarm that the water seemed to be rising almost every day. On some of the atolls, the highest point of land was only about ten feet above sea level. With water rising two feet, the buffer between the dune line and the ocean disappeared. Rainstorms would routinely flood the islands.

Fortunately, most of these islands were sparsely inhabited, allowing local authorities to evacuate the islands to larger home ports when major storms approached. In 2077, the several score people living on the Aldabra Islands in the Indian Ocean were evacuated in the face of a churning cyclone. A ferry picked them up and took them back to the Seychelle islands to ride out the storm.

Three days later, the storm had passed and the ship loaded up the Aldabrans to return them to their island, best known for its population of giant tortoises. When they arrived at the area where the islands had been, three of the atolls no longer existed. The waves and the storm had completely obliterated the islands.

Similar disasters occurred in the Maldive Islands, southwest of India, only in many cases not only did the islands vanish, so did hundreds of people living on them.

Nature aimed its most ruthless and devastating blast at the fertile lowlands of India and Bangladesh, territory that Mother Nature has visited with awesome displays of natural fury. Undeterred by rising waters, the Bangladeshi and Indians in the great river deltas of the Asian subcontinent simply built higher and higher earthen dikes around the silt-formed river islands upon which land-starved villagers could set up ramshackle homes and till the rich earth to produce three or four crops a year.

Even when there wasn't a storm, thousands of villagers and farmers would suddenly be killed when these dams, often constructed without the benefit of government approval, would collapse without warning. The farmland was already several feet below sea level. When the dike failed, death would occur almost instantly, as the ocean would reclaim the spot of earth in minutes.

In 2102, however, one of the all-too-frequent Indian Ocean cyclones, packing winds in excess of 150 miles an hour and pushing a storm surge twenty-five feet high swept up the Bay of Bengal. Hundreds of villages disappeared; water scoured the port of Chittagong, where four million people lived; the water surged up the delta, flooding the capital city of Dhaka and its twelve million people. When the waters receded and authorities assessed the extent of the disaster, it was estimated that six million people had perished.

The shaken Bangladesh government, stunned by a disaster that they could not have prevented or even mitigated, declared that all land within five miles of the ocean or less than twenty-five feet above sea level was to be abandoned, effectively reducing the arable land and living space by twenty-five percent, crowding the population of one of the most crowded nations in the world even closer together.

Even after the disaster, Bangladesh had 168 million people, who now lived in an area the size of West Virginia. The main cities of Chittagong and Dhaka were abandoned as well, along with the most modern services, universities, and medical facilities. The worst of contagious and deadly diseases befell the population: Malaria, dengue, cholera, typhus attacked with horrible results, killing hundreds of thousands of people a week.

Even responses by the best efforts of relief agencies failed to make a dent in the disaster. Huge areas of the country were quarantined in hopes of limiting the outbreaks, but the people in the area who were not sick pushed out of the enclaves, defying soldiers to shoot them. The soldiers stepped aside and the mass of refugees, many of whom were incubating disease, poured out into the uninfected countryside.

Wave after wave of pandemics followed, killing people faster than graves could be dug. Bonfires of the dead blazed day and night, and were so commonplace around the country that citizens on the Moon could identify the borders of Bangladesh by the ring of fires in the night. The string of disasters continued for fifteen years, reducing the Bangladesh population to ninety-six million people, by official census, in 2117.

"Just an increase of two feet of water did that?" I said, exhausted by the narration of the Guide, who showed me pictures of the horror in Bangladesh.

"That's just part of the story. By the early part of the twenty-second century, the world was too much of a community village for one part not to be affected by something occurring half a world away," he intoned almost deity-like.

The Guide's words had mesmerized me so completely, I'd forgotten we were still watching the anguished scenes in the St. Louis hospital in the twenty-second century.

"I'm confused. I see that the rising waters of the oceans would have an impact on coastal communities, especially in low-lying areas around the world. And disease is a problem that has been rampant in undeveloped countries since mankind started gathering in towns and cities. What's happening with St. Louis? Why is there an outbreak of tropical disease here? What am I missing?"

"For this story we have to go back in time to the mid-1950s when polio was the most terrible disease in existence. The polio virus struck down young Americans with frightening speed and devastating results. Young boys and girls were paralyzed, their arms and legs withered, adults' lungs didn't function, and people spent years in iron lungs. Children were warned to avoid garbage, trash, friends, animals. And then Jonas Salk came up with his vaccine, and deaths and disability from polio vanished virtually overnight."

I remembered. I was one of those children who were among the hundreds of thousands who were part of the polio vaccine experiment. I winced as I thought of those dull needles through which the life-saving vaccine was administered. Two years later I found out they had inoculated me with purple water, and I had to take the series of shots again. But then I didn't get polio, and I can't remember that any of my friends came down with the disease either.

The Guide lectured on, spreading his hands in front of him as one scene after another illustrated his discussion. In the 1960s, scientists decided that they could beat one of

Mother Nature's historically vicious diseases: Smallpox. In a worldwide effort spurred by the World Health Organization, scientists tracked every single outbreak of smallpox and inoculated everything that moved anywhere near where the cases were identified. In 1979, after inoculating millions of people in the Horn of Africa—the area around the Sudan, Somalia, and Ethiopia—victory over smallpox was declared. Except for a couple of vials maintained in government laboratories, small pox had been eliminated.

In 1979, doctors believed that for the first time in the 3.5 billion years that bacteria and viruses had inhabited the Earth, the bacteria were on the run. Mankind had beaten the bugs, and we should look forward to one success after another, until we could have a bug-free world. There were even professors at major universities who said the funding of laboratories to study virology would be a waste of time because by the millennium the bugs would be in full retreat.

The Guide looked around. "The optimists saw the Ebola virus epidemic in 1976 as an anomaly. They ignored the threats posed by Lassa Valley fever and other minor outbreaks of deadly diseases that occurred in faraway places and killed a few dozen or a few hundred people and then vanished from the news—if they even made the news. After all, how important are the deaths of a few villagers in Africa when Roseanne is divorcing another husband.

"Of course, then came AIDS, and suddenly those that didn't see a need for virologists started placing frantic ads for them."

Scientists made great strides in technology: the development of magnetic resonance imaging to visualize internal body organs without surgery or catheters; locating the receptors on cells that made it possible to reduce cholesterol with a pill or fight cancer with a direct attack on out-of-control cells.

But they were losing the ground against the bugs. Doctors fell in love with antibiotics when they became available in the 1930s, especially after World War II, when penicillin became the medicine of choice to fight lung and other infections.

The bad thing about penicillin is that it worked too well.

Within a couple of days of administration, stubborn lung infections that had troubled patients for weeks virtually vanished. As the word spread about this miracle drug, every time a child sniffled a pediatrician would prescribe penicillin. If the pediatrician showed restraint, parents would shop for a practitioner who would order the drug.

By the 1980s, it became apparent that something was wrong with penicillin. It no longer knocked out infections as it used to do. The reason was simple: when someone was sick with a lung infection, billions of bacteria cells were busy replicating and attacking the tissue. If the body's own defenses came up short, the patient died.

But with penicillin, the powerful antibiotic went to work on the colonies of bacteria and destroyed them en masse. Within hours the effects were noticeable, the numbers of bacteria dropped by a log—about ninety percent. The patient immediately felt a whole lot better. The next day's dose of the drug killed off another log—ninety percent of what remained, and so on. After ten days of medication, whatever bugs were left were quickly hunted down, absorbed and destroyed by the body's defenses—now strong enough to do the job.

The problem was that after a day or two people felt fine and when you feel fine you don't see any need to take medication. If you feel fine for seven days, the likelihood that you will keep taking this medication decreases further. So people failed—in huge numbers—to complete the course of medication. Inside the body, the hardiest of the bugs, those that had survived the two-, three-, and four-log reductions of bacteria stayed alive. They were constantly multiplying and were on the run from the body's macrophages—the cells that hunt down cells and bugs that shouldn't be in the body. The game of hide-and-seek goes on continually, with the macrophages keeping the bugs in check—until something happens to reduce the body's immune defenses, cigarette smoking—the Guide glared at me—severe trauma, alcohol, any number of things.

Now the bug that should have been eradicated by the penicillin begins to produce in numbers that cannot be controlled by a weakened immune system, and the infection reemerges in clinical strength. The patient returns to the doctor who again orders penicillin—but the penicillin doesn't work nearly as well—the bugs have become resistant.

By the year 2000, penicillin was almost worthless against vast numbers of diseases. Second-line antibiotics were losing the war against certain pneumonia bacteria. There were even some really nasty bugs that were resistant to vancomycin, the most powerful antibiotic on the planet at the time.

These vancomycin-resistant enterococci (known as VREs) created havoc in hospitals throughout the early twenty-first century. The VREs were responsible for up to twenty-five percent of infections acquired in the hospital. That meant you went into the hospital to have your appendix removed and while you were recuperating one of these VREs got into that wound in your side and began multiplying like crazy. By the time doctors figured out why you were suddenly close to death, they also figured out that there was nothing they could do to save you.

It was as if you had crawled into a time machine and had crawled out the other end in 1922, with nothing available to assist your fight for life. By 2004, patients infected with VREs were dying in more than half the cases. It's not that the bug was particularly virulent, but if it hit you in the hospital, it was hitting someone who was already sick, with a reduced immune system. If the bug found its way into a severely immunocompromised patient—someone undergoing chemotherapy for cancer or a patient with AIDS, the battle was over quickly. The bug won.

Even for those relatively healthy patients—like the appendicitis victim—the battle was pitched. The hospital administered fluids and nutrients to give the patient a fighting chance, but the death rate from VREs was well above forty percent. The presence of VREs led to a marked increase in the use of home-infusion therapies, even for very ill cancer patients. Chemotherapy given at home was seen as a way to keep as many compromised patients out of the hospital as possible because the hospital was a natural breeding ground for these diseases.

When numbers of patients began showing up at emergency rooms or in doctors' private offices suffering from internal stomach disorders that didn't respond to any antibiotics, the health profession realized that the VREs were in the community—that is, you could catch one of these resistant bugs by being in the same classroom, bus, airplane, or supermarket with someone else who had the disease. And it didn't matter if you had always completed your medication as prescribed—if you were infected with one of these VREs, the bug was just as resistant to medicine as the ones found in hospitals in previously ill patients. And you were just as likely to die as anyone else.

It took until 2008 before pharmaceutical companies could create an effective next level of antibiotics that brought the Great VRE Epidemic to a halt. The health profession, having seen the antibug euphoria dissipate into reality, continued hard at work in the laboratory attempting to create the next higher level of antibiotics and a level after that. Researchers now knew that an antibiotic was good for maybe twenty years before resistance to it emerged. And it only took another twenty years after that for the drug to become almost worthless in the battle against the bacteria.

The fight against viruses encountered similar problems. Antibiotics don't work on viruses. What are needed are antiviral medications, some of which work fairly well; others don't work well at all.

In industrialized communities, most often areas located in temperate climates, the viruses are relatively easy to cope with, except for an infrequent but virulent strain of influenza. "You should read about the great influenza epidemic of 1918 so you are familiar with that health mystery before it's solved," the Guide said.

"What was so mysterious about it?" I asked.

"No one knows what strain of influenza caused it."

"But you said it would be solved?"

"Remind me to talk to you about that some other time." He put his finger across his lips and continued with his history lesson on viruses. It sounded so erudite coming

from someone dressed in a loincloth and an open deerskin
vest.

In the United States, the Ebola virus made for interesting
movies and interesting reading for people who could get
vicarious thrills from reading about death and uncontrol-
lable illness in some unpronounceable village in Zaire. It
was thrilling reading about the body counts, seeing the pictures of the grieving families, experiencing the prurient interest in CNN live reports of burning bodies in mass graves.

Not too many people outside the medical community
seemed to care that no one ever found the suspected animal
reservoir—the creature that carried the virus. That meant
the virus could erupt again someday. No one outside that
concerned health community cared that the DNA analysis
of the Ebola outbreak in 1976 was precisely the same as
the one in Kikwit in 1995. Both outbreaks killed eighty
percent of the humans it infected. No one seemed concerned that no medicine known to mankind had any effect
on Ebola at all—and no one was working on any vaccine
or antiviral agent to combat the bug either. There was very
little discussion about the fact that the original Ebola fever
outbreak occurred in a village in the Ebola River Valley,
in northern Zaire, not far from the border of the Central
African Republic. The second Ebola outbreak was in Kikwit—more than five hundred miles from the Ebola Valley.
Yet the same virus was responsible for both outbreaks. Not
a similar virus; the same virus. It seemed likely that the
reservoir for the virus was not the same animal, and whatever animals had the virus were spreading it across equatorial Africa. Then in 1996, there was a smaller outbreak
in Gabon, to the west of the Ebola River Valley.

When scientists from the Centers for Disease Control in
Atlanta sat down and started to draw a picture of the possible spread of Ebola virus, the meetings were grim.

In front of me in that hospital corridor—where another
room had been emptied as a gurney with a sheet-covered
body was wheeled toward the end of the hallway, and another groaning patient replaced the dead one—a hologram
of Africa appeared.

The Guide highlighted the Ebola River Valley and Kikwit. Conservatively it took sixteen years for the virus to migrate from Ebola to Kikwit, assuming, of course, that Ebola was actually the epicenter of the outbreak. In another fifteen years, all of equatorial Africa would have been invaded by animals carrying the virus. He pointed to the hills in Nigeria, Tanzania, and Angola.

Most likely, he continued, the higher elevations prevented the spread of the disease. Whatever animal carried Ebola it must have been a creature that liked the lowlands because subsequent outbreaks—my eyes widened—occurred in tropical areas. Most of the new outbreaks in the early twenty-first century were identified rapidly and the disease was restricted to fewer than ten people. As a consequence reports rarely made the evening news and were restricted to medical journals. Until the Hadj Epidemic.

In 2024, a devout Islamic peasant from a jungle village in Nigeria boards a jumbo jet in Lagos to make the pilgrimage to Mecca. The man, a woodcutter, had saved pennies since he was thirteen to be able to afford the pilgrimage to Mecca, fulfilling the Muslim requirement to make one visit to the holy sites of his religion in his lifetime. The fifty-five-year-old man, although feeling feverish, boards the plane with 480 other passengers crammed into the chartered creaky, but still serviceable, 747.

Midway in the five-hour flight the man becomes violently ill. Numerous other pilgrims struggle to make him comfortable as he sweats, vomits blood, and suffers convulsions and seizures on the plane. Although Ebola virus cannot be spread through the air, enough contact with fellow passengers is made to allow the virus to penetrate the skin of others. A dozen other people are infected before the plane lands in Mecca.

During bouts of consciousness the man pleads with his fellow pilgrims to be taken to the sacred shrines of Mecca before being hospitalized, fearing he will miss his chance to be nearer to Allah. He is covered with blankets to stifle the chills and is carried by other Muslims to the sacred monuments of the faith. Scores of others who come in contact with the Nigerian are infected.

As his symptoms worsen, the Nigerian is brought to a

modern Saudi Arabian hospital. The asymptomatic others board planes which take them home to every continent on Earth (one resident of a facility on the Moon is discovered as being infected before his flight home leaves).

When laboratory tests in Mecca confirm that the Nigerian had the Ebola virus, bug detectives from around the world converge on Saudi Arabia and the travel records of every major airline and charter facility serving the religious center. Another team goes to Nigeria to track down the virus from the Nigerian's village.

Eventually close to a thousand Ebola deaths will be attributed to this one case and world governments will spend three years and a quarter billion dollars in a frantic attempt to track down the virus carriers before the infections can be spread.

The result will be frustrating: In all cases the Ebola virus will be identical to the one which caused the outbreak fifty years earlier in Zaire; researchers will glumly declare that the virus can survive in the body of a human even if that human lives in a temperate climate (something they expected but about which they hoped they would be wrong); that the disease is just as virulent as before—seventy-nine percent of those infected die of the disease; that nothing in the arsenals of the world's pharmacies can cope with the virus; and, worst of all, the animal reservoir harboring the virus is still unidentified.

My mouth was agape as he finished the story, and the little bright spots on the world globe dimmed and even the holographic globe disappeared. "But what about St. Louis and his water?" I questioned gently.

"Actually," he said, "high water had nothing to do with it. The *Aedes aegypti* is the real culprit. The mosquito which carried dengue."

I grew up in Brooklyn and lived all my life in New York City. A trip to Atlantic City is what I consider going South, although I will admit to a few trips to Miami Beach in my misspent youth.

"What is dengue fever?" I asked.

"It's the worst case of flu that you will ever get. You will be nauseous; you'll vomit; you'll sweat; you will feel as if someone has beaten your body black-and-blue or that you've run a marathon; you will be dizzy; you'll be sick as hell. And you likely will not die—the first time.''

The real problem with dengue fever is that once you get the disease you are immune to the strain of dengue you acquire: four strains of the disease exist. If you then contract any of the other strains, you will come down with dengue hemorrhagic fever, a deadly disease. Dengue hemorrhagic fever is so deadly that thirty to forty percent of the people who contract the disease, unless they receive aggressive treatment to maintain body strength, will die from the disease within a few days. Fortunately, in modern facilities where adequate water supplies are available, the death rate can be reduced to around 5 percent.

"Uh, five percent is one out of twenty. My rule of thumb in worrying about things is that if the odds are so great you would never win at the race track, you don't have to worry about it getting you," I explained to the Guide. "I've had a lot of twenty to one shots pay off for me. That means this is a really scary disease in the best of places.''

The Guide nodded. "In the best of facilities, in the best of conditions, with the best of care. When the epidemic hits doctors and nurses and orderlies and technicians and attendants and emergency medical workers at the same time, the best of conditions no longer exists. And that death rate zooms.''

In the year-of-no-winter 2113, the *Aedes aegypti* mosquito migrated north of Memphis, supposedly the limit of its range, followed the Mississippi River up to St. Louis, then rode along the banks of the Missouri past St. Joseph— the original start of the Oregon Trail—before it felt air chilly enough to make it turn tail. Along the way, the mosquito dropped its eggs. Some of the mosquitoes already harbored the dengue virus and infected people all along the river. Most of the victims of the fever stayed at home and waited a couple of agonizing weeks while the disease ran its course. But the aggressive mosquitoes kept biting and spreading the disease.

The year-of-no winter 2113, in which temperatures never dipped below forty degrees, was followed by a warm, humid summer and another relatively warm winter of 2114. The winter of 2116 was the fourth year in a row of balmy temperatures as far north as Springfield, Illinois. But by that spring, a second strain of dengue had been carried by mosquitoes up the Mississippi Valley and the epidemic of dengue hemorrhagic fever spread over the countryside in wave after wave.

Those who didn't have the means of travel, the money, or support of relatives couldn't get to the hospitals for treatment. And since entire families were usually infected simultaneously, often everyone in a household was dead or dying before the meager available help found them. The fever didn't play favorites: Whoever the mosquito bit was felled by the disease.

"There is no treatment for dengue fever today except for nutritional and liquid support," the Guide said. "There won't be any treatment in 2116 either. The toll will be devastating. Tens of thousands will die, and government's only answer will be diligence in mosquito-eradication projects. Those projects had been under way before, but now it was obvious that more funds would have to be spent in controlling the bugs. Like any good democracy, the reaction will be sufficient to keep the problem under control for another few decades. But the range of the mosquito will spread as long as the Earth gets warmer, and the weather will get warmer yet."

21

A MEDICAL NIGHTMARE COVERS THE GLOBE

I GOT PEEKS OF THE GRAY BACKDROP INTERMITTENTLY AS the snow streamed into my face, sometimes so thick even the grayish sky and the dark wood of the barren trees faded into a giant white plasterboard. The blizzard was so heavy I tried to use my arms as windshield wipers in front of my face, and was astounded to see that I wasn't wearing any gloves. I wasn't even wearing a coat. I turned my hands toward my face and stared at them as if they weren't part of my body. I wondered, also, *How come I'm not freezing? If all this snow is hitting my face, why isn't my face cold? If the wind is howling like a banshee, why can't I feel it on my face?*

Of course, I knew why. I was dreaming. I reached out for the covers on my bed, and flailed away, seeking the light on the bedside table without success.

''The Guide!'' I remembered. The other possibility. I tried to find him, but he could have been inches away and I couldn't have seen him in the blizzard. I turned quickly to either side and suddenly I knew what happened in white-

167

out conditions. The horizon had disappeared. I thought I was standing up but I could have been lying down or crawling. The swirling whiteness cracked and I spotted the dark brown legs of the Guide, his feet set squarely apart, the snow up to his knees. I righted myself.

"Siberia?" It certainly satisfied my idea of what Siberia in a snowstorm would appear.

The Guide gave me one of those "how-did-you-know" looks, and nodded.

"I was just joking," I yelled above the noise of the storm.

"Good," he said. "If you start to read my mind, they'll make me go help someone else."

"They?"

"Forget it." It wasn't a request. I forgot it.

"So, Siberia. What are we doing in Siberia?"

"Watch and learn."

He was getting rather formal. Maybe he was concerned that I could read his mind as he could read mine. I peered at him covertly. He was focused at the tree line, about thirty yards ahead.

I followed his gaze. At first I saw nothing, but then there was movement. A dark shape—a bear, perhaps—stumbled between the trees and then sank to its knees. Now I could see that the form was human, but I couldn't make out whether it was a man or woman. I stared more intently. Ah, a man. He had a beard. He pulled a tool out of his backpack—a folding shovel—and began digging into the snow. He dug frantically, piling up walls on either side of him, then he began burrowing under the walls.

I'd read enough Jack London in my youth to understand the desperate man's motives. He was going to build a snow fort, lie inside, and let his body's warmth fill the fort—the snow would provide insulation, and he could ride out the blizzard. The only drawbacks were the possibility that the storm would last too long and he'd freeze to death anyway, and the problem of what he was going to do for food.

The man's action stopped abruptly, and the snow piled up higher and higher. The storm continued unabated, then slowed in intensity and stopped. It could have been an hour or a day or a week. These travels with the Guide telescoped time. Since most of our travels had been to the future, I accepted that we were deep in the twenty-first century, but snow was snow. I waited.

A tree branch snapped. The sun was shining but I could tell that even with the brilliance with which the rays danced on the snow, the warming effects of the sun weren't going to make a lot of difference in this scene. I felt cold even though I could not feel cold. I saw movement near the tree line and watched in wonder as the snow shook and moved and the man emerged from his underground shelter. His breath produced a white cloud every time he exhaled and he exhaled frequently, meaning the air was so cold he could not take a sharp inhale of the frigid air.

He stomped around, shaking the snow from his heavy jacket. He seemed uncertain about what to do next. He let his eyes circle his domain 360 degrees, pausing a bit to look directly at us, then moving on. He struggled over to the trees and flattened an area, then dropped his pants and turned away from us. A stream of steam rose up from the area in front of him, which we could not see.

"Modest," the Guide mumbled.

The man pulled up his clothes quickly and trudged back to his fortress of snow. He pulled a device from his backpack. He pressed a button on the six-inch-long tube and a rod about three feet long shot out. The man flattened out another space about ten feet into the open area and slammed the pointed end of the shaft into the snow. It crunched to a halt. He pressed another button and a fanlike device opened up. The man reached into his backpack again and came out with a palm-sized square with an electric plug on the end and inserted it into the space on the shaft. He waited a few seconds, and tapped a few digits into a handheld calculator. He pulled the device out of the snow and marched another ten feet and reimplanted it, repeating the measurements.

I gave the Guide an "okay-tell-me-what's-going-on" shrug.

"The device picks up a signal from a navigational satellite that tells him precisely where he is on Earth. It's similar to the loran navigational devices that boaters use to figure out where the shore is in fog and storms and where the good fishing spots are located. He's making successive markings so he knows what direction to follow.''

"Can a signal from space be that accurate?"

"This is a commercial satellite used for buses, cars, and travelers in the twenty-second century. It's only accurate up to six inches. The military ones can be used to direct a laser that can open a can of tuna on the surface without singeing the grass around it.''

The man gathered up his device and returned to his snow fort. Just outside the fort he slammed the shaft into the snow again, to hold it until he repacked his possessions. But instead of the expected "kechunnnk" sound of penetrating hardened snow and frost, the shaft made a convincing "thunk," the sound of steel hitting wood. But not the sound you'd expect to hear when hitting a tree root or log. More like impact with something that had seen the work of a carpenter. The man showed surprise, yanked the shaft out, then replaced it a few inches away. The same sound. He repeated the action again.

He left the shaft sticking up into the snow, like some strange metallic flower crafted by a visiting spaceman, and climbed back into the fort, reemerging with his shovellike instrument, and began clearing snow and ice from the area around the shaft.

"This is how it begins, Shawn. This is it."

A wave of nausea swept through me as if I had just been told of gross atrocities committed against mankind.

The Guide nodded as if he knew my thoughts.

"It's been here for centuries—buried in ice and snow and forgotten—its power for destruction not even conceived. Mother Nature is going to show the residents of the twenty-second century who's boss, once again," the Guide said. "Man's arrogance will again be his downfall."

In the freezing temperatures of Siberia, the survivor of the storm methodically shoveled and scraped away snow from the area where he heard the wooden sounds. Every fifteen minutes or so he would duck back into his snow house, then return to his work. The object was buried under about three feet of loose snow, packed snow, and crusted ice. The man's beard was now a mass of ice, formed by the condensation of his breath. He gazed anxiously at the sun, which was perilously low in the sky. The entire period of daylight was only about five hours, and he hadn't climbed out of the snow house until after the sun had already been up for a couple of hours. He paused to calculate what he would have to do and came to the conclusion that another night under the snow was his only option. He had wasted too much time at the site, and there wasn't enough daylight for him to reach his next haven on foot. He pulled out a small plasticlike sheet and spread it over his work area to prevent drifting snow or another storm from covering his excavation, weighing down the corners of the sheet with blocks of hard-packed snow that he had chopped from his dig. He pushed other blocks into the snow house and crawled inside, using the blocks to seal himself inside the house for another night.

Even before the sun had crept over the horizon, the man was back at his work the next day. He found one edge of the wooden object and worked along it to a corner, then found a second corner about eighteen inches away. He was able to make out markings on the object, so he became more careful to avoid damaging the artwork further. He rued his crude attacks on the object, finding holes where the shaft of his locator had struck the wood.

His mind was working all fronts, clearing the snow, preserving the object and trying to figure out what it was that was being uncovered. At first he thought it was a table, but it had solid sides that were about two feet long. He had an idea about the dimension of the object and quickly located the third and fourth corners. He stared at it and then recoiled: a coffin.

He considered the find, noting with interest that the design seemed similar to descriptions of coffins that had been commonplace in the mid-1800s. This coffin was three hundred years old! *How could it have survived so long,* he thought, quickly reckoning that the cold must have preserved it. His excavations found something else. The coffin seemed to rest on a rusted frame of a sledge. He rested and contemplated what he was working on. He thought, *There was a funeral party that was taking this coffin to a grave. It was winter because the coffin was being pulled by a sledge. They reached the forest, but never got a chance to bury the coffin. Were they attacked by wolves? Were they attacked by roving bandits? Were they beset by a sudden snowstorm and decided to leave the coffin and return to finish the burial another day? Did that possible snowstorm hide the coffin and it could never be located? Where did they come from? There wasn't a village within fifty miles of the area? Perhaps there was one at the time?*

He shrugged and continued to excavate. He realized that luck had given him a great find. Inside the coffin would be artifacts of an ancient time, and the market for these objects was very large. Russian artifacts, especially primitive Russian art and icons, were selling like hotcakes. The weakness of the Russian government as it played a Ping-Pong game between socialism and capitalism meant there were very little controls on the black market sales of artifacts, the reason the man was searching the wilderness of northern Siberia in the first place. It was one area that hadn't been plundered by other professionals in the field.

He and others had been accused of being nothing but glorified or criminal grave robbers. He smiled, cracking some ice from his reddened cheeks. "This isn't grave robbing. This never made it to a grave," he said as he felt for the nails or wooden pegs that were meant to seal the coffin. He decided to take whatever was of value from the coffin and carry it back to his base. He knew the exact location of the coffin and could come back with machinery or a helicopter to remove it, once he convinced backers who had access to that type of machinery that it was worth the expense. He would cover the coffin with snow again and pray that no one else stumbled across it.

He carefully removed one of the pins and searched for the others, found that despite four hundred years of exposure, the cold had preserved the coffin and its working parts. He was excited now, realizing that nothing in the coffin was likely to have been irretrievably damaged. He thought of the icons that would have been buried with the dead, the embroidered shroud, possibly even bracelets or jewels. It could be worth a fortune. He might never have to go on one of these bitter hunts again.

From his pack he pulled out his self-heating knife and slid it all around the lid of the coffin. As he completed the circuit around the box, he could feel the lid give. Carefully he slid it back and looked inside.

The corpse was still intact. Although it had not decayed, the body was sere. The water in the body had disappeared and evaporated over the centuries. The man assumed from the shroud that the body was that of a woman. Her hair was long and blond. But he didn't know whether that was a natural color or had something to do with discoloration. The skin was pulled taut over the bone structure, so it wasn't possible to get an idea of whether the woman had been attractive or plain or scarred. The man didn't pay much attention. He was more interested in the other objects in the coffin. The shroud was linen, white and delicately embroidered. He knew it was valuable in the twenty-second century market, but he also recognized that it was frozen into the folds of the body. He was going to need further expertise to remove it. He glumly thought that he was going to have to sell the body with its shroud to a museum. And museums did not pay the kind of fee he felt was deserved for such a rare find.

However, there were enough other items in the coffin that made his eyes glow. Over the woman's legs was a gorgeous quilt, neatly folded. Even after centuries the color of the religious drawings was still sharp. He knew that with cleaning it would fetch tens of thousands of rubles—or thousands of dollars, yen, or marks, depending on the bidder. It was frozen solid. He tried to see if it was attached to the corpse. He wiggled his gloved hand under the quilt and tried to move it. It shifted easily. He used his other hand to hold the shroud and slowly lifted the quilt. When he was certain that the quilt no longer touched the shroud, he lifted it up, noting with satisfaction that the shroud was still intact. Body liquids followed the law of gravity. The shroud stuck to the body, but did not affect the quilt.

He carried the quilt to an open spot on the snow and wrapped it in another plastic sheet, which emerged from a small pack to its full five-foot-by-five-foot size. He turned his attention to the rest of the objects in the coffin. There were several wooden icons of the Madonna. Rubles rang in his head. There were numerous piles of clothing in the corners of the coffin. He removed them and placed them in other plastic sheets. Under one of the piles of clothing was a small carved box. Excitedly, but with a jeweler's hand control, he worked the box open and was rewarded with the sight of several gold and silver bracelets and necklaces.

"Oh wonderful God," he prayed out loud, looking up into the startling blue skies. "How you have smiled upon me."

He finished his chores, cleaning out the coffin, which contained far more items than he would have suspected. He barely wondered about why this corpse was going to her grave with so many possessions but let that thought pass as he considered how much wealth this one failure to bury was going to be worth to him.

The sun was setting once again, so the man carried his loot into the temporary snow house to wait until the morrow, when he would trek to his base and plan for selling his merchandise.

The sun sank and darkness settled over the Siberian scene. Despite the sky being lit up by millions of stars, the ground was bleak and dark. The starlight soon faded as well, replaced by a fog and drizzle and the muffled hum of motor vehicles, one of which had Cyrillic lettering and the outward look of an emergency vehicle, sirens and flashing strobe lights. The vehicle rolled to a stop in front of a sleek building, also with the letters that place it in Russia or one of the Eastern European nations using that language.

The Guide translated what was happening, explaining that the scene is indeed in Moscow in a major teaching hospital. It is June 2155. The ambulance door opens and a gurney transports the feverish patient down the corridor to an emergency treatment area. Doctors and nurses come in and examine the patient. He's feverish, in pain, complaining about not being able to see. His face, back, and neck are covered with hideous, pus-oozing sores. His legs and sides were covered with large red blotches.

Doctors began taking blood and saliva samples and sent them to the laboratory for analysis. Three hours later the report came back: Unknown virus. The doctors were stymied and weren't going to get much help from the patient, who had died before the report was returned.

The report was filed away with exhortations to doctors to be on the alert for others with the same symptoms. In the meantime, the unknown virus report was sent to the hospital's databank processor to be sent to Atlanta, Georgia, in the United States, where the U.S. Centers for Disease Control kept tabs on new illnesses. The outbreaks in the twenty-first century involving drug-resistant microbes, the horrendous Ebola outbreak, and the more recent dengue disaster were enough for world governments to be alert to any new microbe that was lying in wait for human victims.

Three days later, a keen-eyed epidemiologist at the CDC matched the report from Moscow with something similar in Finland, and another report out of Kazakhstan that also seemed to be the same problem.

She received funding and permission to visit the Russian hospital, arriving there another seven days later—and in the middle of a mushrooming epidemic. Fifteen doctors, nurses, orderlies, and porters at the hospital were all suffering from the strange disease, already nine people had died. A surgeon had gone blind, but seemed to be surviving; the ambulance attendant suffered horribly, but lived and had deep scars on his face to prove it.

The CDC worker moved among the victims of the disease, something in the back of her brain gave her the answer as she walked down the hospital corridor. The thought overwhelmed her and she collapsed in the hallway. Hospital staff members rushed to her side, but she shooed them away. She steadied herself and stumbled and shook as she got to the administrator's office of the hospital and, interrupting a meeting, demanded that she be given the administrator's personal skylink phone.

She snatched the phone from the hands of the startled administrator and tapped out the numbers, realizing that the

voice-response mechanism undoubtedly knew just Russian.
Her boss picked up the emergency beeper at 5 A.M. Atlanta
time, noted that it was the researcher in Moscow, and mumbled a barely audible, "Hello."

"Dan, Dan," she cried, "It's smallpox! Smallpox! I
know it's not possible, but that's what it is, I'm sure of it."
Her voice quieted. "Dan, I think I'm dead."

In 1979, researchers for the World Health Organization
announced that smallpox, a plague on the planet that had
been identified by scholars as long ago as the fourth century, had been eradicated forever.

Being human, however, governments still required smallpox vaccinations for another ten to fifteen years because
just because the WHO said the disease was eradicated
didn't necessarily mean the disease was eradicated. By the
start of the twenty-first century, even in the most conser-
vative of medical departments at one time, the most small-
pox-ridden underdeveloped countries were giving in and
not requiring the vaccinations for admission to their countries. By 2040, virtually every hospital in the world had
discarded their smallpox-vaccine caches.

Smallpox itself has no successful treatment, and as late
as 1950, as many as ten percent of the people who developed smallpox died of the disease. In some populations
virulent strains of the disease killed two-thirds of its victims.

"Do you remember Kateri Tekakwitha?" the Guide
asked suddenly.

The waves of that colorful aura struck me again like a
tsunami. "Of course, I remember," I told him. "Kateri is
the reason I am here."

"And one of the reasons Kateri was recognized as a special person touched by the Holy One was the epidemic of
smallpox that ravaged her village and killed her parents and
brother and left her pockmarked and nearly blind.

"Her injuries, however, enhanced her ability to see the
future, much as you can, Shawn."

He returned to his narrative of the Great Smallpox Epidemic of 2151.

Simone Jackson's favorite pastime while working between epidemics at the CDC was to go back into the archives and follow how the great doctors of the past had dealt with the bizarre in the field of illness. She had studied the Ebola outbreaks; the hantavirus disasters in the twenty-first century; even the ancient cholera outbreaks. And she had marveled at the success in eradicating smallpox (1979); polio (2017); and the sexually transmitted disease chlamydia (2043).

Now as she used her hospital room as a command center she expected that smallpox, a disease that had been eradicated 150 years before she was born, was going to kill her. *How did I step into this time machine?* she asked herself. She knew she had about a week before the fever started; then a couple of days when the pimples would form. If she could keep from scratching at them, perhaps they would not spread throughout her body. Maybe, she'd be lucky enough just to be scarred for life. Simone had always been proud of her smooth skin. She vowed that if she survived this, no matter how she survived, she'd find some plastic surgeon who would be able to repair her face. The gene surgeons could perform miracles. But now she needed a miracle from another source.

Using computers and telephones, Jackson was able to backtrack and try to locate how this new scourge had been loosed on the planet. She was mystified by the fact that the only reported occurrences were in northern climates: Finland, Moscow, Zhaltyr in Kazakhstan, near the Russian border.

Once the word got out—it could hardly be kept a secret—that smallpox was again among the population, the news channels tried to outdo themselves in finding out where it originated. Now that the disease was identified, the reports started pouring in from all over the world: London, Tokyo, Tel Aviv, New Ankara. Jackson was stunned by the number of reports and wondered why these reports, some of which were forty-five days old, had not been reported to the CDC. In her heart she knew why—people just couldn't be bothered.

She demanded that the families of the known victims of the disease be checked, and in almost every case one, two, or three members of the family had died of the mysterious ailment or were suffering from its consequences. After a couple of days, Jackson had found a link. Three of the victims had recently visited Norilsk, an industrial town in Siberia, known as a hot spot in the illicit trade of Russian art works.

A Russian-U.S. expedition jetted to Norilsk and found chaos in the medical institutions. Hospitals were closed because medical staffs were dead or dying. Thousands of people were suffering in their homes. Scores had been burned alive by terrified citizens who didn't know what was happening but their ancient instincts told them what to do about it.

Jackson, when told of the slaughter, inwardly praised the torchers who might actually help stem the epidemic. But she also knew that there was not going to be any way of getting the genie back into the bottle.

The strain of smallpox that was out, as fate would have it, was one of the particularly virulent ones. It was loose in a population that was almost totally open to the infection— a population that didn't have a drop of vaccine available.

Once the word was out that smallpox was loose again, scientists around the world dusted off formulas and began producing the vaccine. They were aided by advances in genetic technology that meant that as soon as the first batch of vaccine was cultured growth factors could be introduced that quickly produced tens of millions of doses of the vaccine.

It won't be enough, thought Jackson, who knew that she would either contract smallpox or not before the vaccine could get to her. She remembered from her research that the way smallpox was handled in the twentieth century was to isolate the smallpox victim and then inoculate every man, woman, or child that was anywhere in the vicinity of that person, and do the same for the next two, three, and four levels of contagion. If one case of smallpox was discovered in a nomadic band, every person in the band was vaccinated and so was every living person that could be found that visited any oasis or trading center that an infected person had visited. One case required twenty thousand vaccinations.

Ten days after she arrived in Moscow, a space-suited CDC volunteer knocked on the door of her enclosed room and vaccinated her against the disease. She was one of thirty-eight people in the hospital who seemed to be uninfected. In the hospital's morgue were 256 bodies. Every bed in the hospital was filled with people in various stages of the illness. Outside it was worse.

The Red Army had been called up to patrol the city of seventeen million people and not allow anyone to leave. Tons of disinfectants were helicoptered into the city and stacked at Red Square. Anyone who had lived with a person who had the disease was advised to disinfect their entire building. Some people simply burned the homes to the ground, oftentimes incinerating the bodies in them. More than once, everyone in the household had died. In Moscow alone, eight million deaths were recorded between the end of 2152 and the time that the unaffected could be vaccinated.

But Moscow was not alone in the aftermath of the epidemic, which swirled around the world twice before it was considered under control in 2160. The death toll was estimated at near six hundred million, an almost unthinkable statistic yet it represented only six percent of the population of the globe.

While the outbreak was under control, it wasn't eradicated.

Jackson never contracted the disease, but dedicated her career to tracking it down, finally succeeding in 2167 when she interviewed the wife of the man who found the body in the Siberian woods. Because the man was so concerned about keeping his artifact find secure and undamaged, he would not let his family touch the items. The quilt and other objects harbored the virus, which had somehow survived the cold and the centuries. Once the artifacts were slowly thawed, the virus sought human hosts, including the discoverer of the coffin.

Even though he was suffering from the fevers that marked the onset of the disease, the man had taken the quilt and other icons to the black market of Norilsk. He sold the items and quickly deposited the cash in a local bank, transferring the money back to his family in a remote Siberian city. That action again saved his family, but doomed the bank teller who handled the money, on which the virus from the man's hands had been deposited.

From the surviving family, Jackson discovered that all of the man's confederates were killed by the disease, and she learned of the location of the mystery coffin. A team of scientists, dressed for an out-of-dome Moon excursion, descended on that copse of trees in Siberia and located the body of the blond-haired woman. Tests proved that the woman had died of smallpox infection circa 1856. Historians would later determine through careful reading of village records that she was allegedly taken to a remote area where she and her possessions were thrown into a grave and incinerated.

Apparently the team sent to eliminate the corpse ran into difficulties because of a snowstorm. They couldn't re-locate the coffin and then fabricated the story of burning the body, assuming that time and the elements would do the job for them.

Instead, six hundred million people would die three hundred years later.

22

FROM THE MINDS
OF CHILDREN COME
WORLD DISASTERS

SOONER OR LATER I KNEW THAT IT HAD TO STOP SNOWING, and that shortly after that the mayor would light a fire under the seat of the public works commissioner and my street in Greenwich Village would be plowed. There was always the outside chance that someone might shovel a path in the snow. However, the better chance was that the temperature would approach normal, a few degrees above the freezing point of water, and the white stuff—now turning a sickish gray—would disappear by itself.

Nevertheless, I also knew that the last of the year-old potpies had been nuked into palatability by the microwave and unless I wanted to share Queenie's unending supply of Meow Mix, it was time to hit the street to forage in the nearest grocery store for what passed as food. I also expected to be gouged by the ever-friendly corner merchant who realized that if a customer stumbled into his store in search of food, a robust increase in the price of that food would not stop the purchase from occurring.

It took me twenty-four hazardous minutes to walk to the corner. I had to dodge sliding cars, cruising snowplows that were hurling tons of slush, ice, and snow at the only possible clearing at the curb, negotiate patches of ice in a style that Sonja Henie would have marveled at, and withstand the gale force winds that city building dynamics created at street corners.

I staggered into the store and grabbed whatever looked reasonably edible and watched in horror as the numbers were flashed on the register. I had one bag of groceries and I needed a new home loan to pay for it. The proprietor smiled graciously as I left; my jaws were clenched in the anger reserved for those who took advantage of mankind in its worst hour. I then retreated to the apartment.

I was only a few steps away when one of the manhole covers in the street belched a plume of condensation mixed with the fine aroma of New York's underground sanitary system. I scrambled to my door and struggled to find my keys as the mist roiled toward me. I thought that I had gotten past the panic attacks. Now the cloud and the smells enveloped me and I could feel my heart go into overdrive. The organ beat like a pile driver, and I wasn't sure how it could pound so hard and still remain in my chest. My throat was dry, yet I could feel perspiration soaking me underneath my coat, sweater, and blouse. Somehow I stumbled into the apartment, plopped my hoard of overpriced food on the floor, threw off my coat, and ran into the bathroom. I grabbed both ends of the sink and steadied myself, panting as if I had just run a marathon.

I turned the faucet and splashed the cool water on my face. Then I screamed as the figure appeared behind me.

"Is this a bad time to talk?" the Guide inquired.

"No," I yelled at him. "I'm fine."

He nodded appreciatively and left the bathroom. It took a few minutes for my heart to stop pounding and for me to get my breathing back to something that approached normalcy. Then I turned back to the living room.

The Guide was sitting cross-legged on the floor, playing with my collection of Lego blocks. I'd had them for ages.

They were fun to play with when I was bored or upset or rattled. Building things calmed me down. I was momentarily envious of the Guide for using the blocks when it was something I would have liked to have done at that moment, but I satisfied my need to do something by putting away the groceries.

He was still constructing a skyscraper when I returned to the room. "Having fun with the Legos?" I asked.

He looked up at me, checking to see if I'd stopped boiling. "Yes," he answered. "They are interesting. And it's not really a toy. You can use the blocks to construct and to enhance your imagination. This is just like the LifeMaker, but these are plastic."

"LifeMaker?"

"Ah, I guess I'm ahead of myself a bit. Want to take a trip with me?"

I didn't bother to answer. I just let myself relax and was subtly aware that everything around me had changed.

In fact, everything around me was in disorder, as if a giant bull had swept through my living room. But then I realized that this wasn't my living room, but someone else's. Destruction abounded. Broken glass represented an aquarium, and tiny fish lay dead on the floor. A bookcase had been shaken, and its contents were scattered about. A chandelier hung by one wire. The window was glassless, the frame askew.

"Tornado?"

He shook his head negatively.

I glanced around again. "Earthquake?"

"Yes." His face twisted angrily. "Here it is 2188 and scientists still haven't figured out how to predict when the Earth will move. Worse, they can't even convince people who live on a fault line that it is not a safe place to reside because the Earth is going to move one day and if you aren't lucky, you will be killed."

"Aren't you being a little tough on people who have just been wiped out?"

He just scowled and pointed to some debris. "Not when such foolishness can destroy the world."

He was gesturing to a room, obviously some child's by the

profusion of sports equipment, dinosaur models—now in several pieces—and torn posters of creatures in bizarre get-ups that must have passed for the latest in rock artists at the end of the twenty-second century. There was a telescope that now resembled a wrapping-paper tube that had been folded in half, a broken microscope, test tubes, slides, and a weird-looking device. I could decipher the name on it: LifeMaker.

"LifeMaker is a toy?"

In 2037, the Guide explained, the Microsoft Cartel expanded again, this time into toy manufacturing by acquiring Mattel. One of the first devices the new brain trust came up with was an inexpensive DNA-sequencing device that really gave grade-school and middle-school students the ability to develop exciting experiments in genetic engineering and identification.

The sequencer revolutionized children's interest in science by giving a child a chance to really learn how life works and how to create, through genetic engineering, improved species.

Although a few budding geniuses came up with some remarkable advances in medical and plant science, most of the experimenting was along the lines of generating ears and toes and hairstyles on poor little mice that were bred to be experimented upon.

The DNA sequencers were relatively simple devices which chemically moved around the four building blocks of life, the amino acids ACGT. Depending on the sequence of those acids and the length of the sequence, everything from an insect to combat tomato blight to a human being could—in theory—be developed. The sequencer, and its surprising "improvements," including the smash hit success of 2096, the artificial Barbie sequencer, became a standard toy for the next century plus.

The sequencer, because it challenged the minds of students over the world, was a gift at almost every age. It was the equivalent of an ever-growing Erector set or train set.

It also was the setting for disaster.

Actually, it was fairly impressive that it took 150 years of use by naive children to come up with something that could be mixed up in a sequencer and create havoc outside the schoolroom laboratory. But it took a relatively small earthquake, a 6.8 Richter-scale tremblor in central California, to result in an Earth-threatening event.

The earthquake's epicenter was on an old, believed dormant fault near King City. The quake moved the Earth's crust two feet across directly under King City's high school, causing the building to collapse in a heap. It also destroyed the city's hospital and wrecked numerous homes. Considering the time of day that it struck, 10:24 A.M. on a Wednesday while school was in session, the fact that only seventeen people were killed, almost all of them at the hospital, was considered miraculous.

The residents of the city decided that no earthquake would force them to move. The wrecked structures were bulldozed and the debris was taken to an area to become the foundation for a waste landfill. What no one realized for several years was that somehow numerous radioactive chemicals used in imaging studies at the hospital were scooped up with the bulldozers and came in contact with numerous school DNA projects, including one in which a student was trying to devise a way of speeding photosynthesis, the process by which plants use sunlight to mature and grow.

In 2206, the landfill was closed, topped with soil, sodded, and fertilized in an oft-tried and generally well-accepted attempt to turn a mountain of trash and garbage into either a park or a golf course or a recreational area. All across the United States, these huge mounds, which dated to the middle of the twentieth century, had been successfully reused. In Florida, several of these landfills vied with each other for the title of "Tallest Point in South Florida." The procedure worked, although many claimed the odor of methane released by the trash as it degraded could still be smelled one hundred years after the last load of trash had been dumped.

A year after the closure of the King City dump, public works personnel were mystified to find that in a large area of the landfill, the sod which had taken root suddenly turned brown and died. The area was dug out, fresh soil was placed in the area and it was resodded. Again the sod died, but the crew noticed a couple of other brown patches emerging around the hillside.

Resodding had no effect, and the browning of the landfill continued. In the spring of 2209, not only was the landfill a wasteland, but areas around the fill were also turning brown. Concerned officials called in experts from state laboratories and they called in researchers in plant genetics, including the world-class plant geneticists from Ohio State University in Columbus.

The Ohio State team harvested samples of the dead grasses and flowers and the soil, sealed them in containers and brought them back to Columbus for study. It took the group months to run the genetic tests and genetic mapping of the plants before they came to a disturbing conclusion. In some manner the photosynthesis of the plants in the area had genetically reversed. More disturbing was the discovery that the gene causing the reversal was a mariner. A mariner is a gene, found in plants and sometimes in lower animals such as insects, which can jump from one species to another and encode itself into the second species. So while the antiphotosynthesis could have begun in one plant species, it had the capability of spreading to others—perhaps all plant species.

In short, the Ohio State researchers said, the possibility of worldwide destruction of its plant life was at hand.

It took a couple of Nobel Prize winners in environmental sciences to explain what that meant in lay terms: First plants will die and along with them all life that depends on plants, like insects, animals, fish in the sea. Plants remove carbon dioxide from the air and return oxygen.

In the early twenty-first century the human barricades that eventually stopped the stripping of the Amazon and other rain forests protested with the plea that the rain forests were the lungs of the Earth.

Without oxygen, the carbon dioxide layer of the Earth would allow for Earth temperatures to increase. The Earth would become hotter and hotter, and eventually the oceans would boil away and soon after so would the atmophere.

How long before that would happen—the boiling away of the atmosphere, people asked. Maybe three hundred to four hundred years, the scientists answered.

Then someone asked: How long in the process before man could no longer survive on the planet.

"We estimate that the rate of growth of the browning, from what we are seeing, should take about seventy-five years for plant life to vanish. Of course, long before then, most of mankind will have perished for lack of food and effects of the poisoning of the atmosphere with carbon dioxide. Unless something is done, mankind will have disappeared by the year 2300," the chief scientist reported matter-of-factly, "about ninety years from now. Of course, I don't think we will be living in a very viable world in fifty years."

It was another asteroid doomsday mission, and in the face of crisis the Earth population knew what to do: Carry on as usual and spend as much money as needed to solve the problem.

The first task was to stop the browning where it now existed. The United States knew how to do that, and although it was illegal according to numerous world treaties, the technology to halt the growth was available and it was in place—high above the world in geostationary orbits.

The first space-based solar power stations went on-line in 2038 and were designed to take solar energy in space and redirect it to solar collectors on Earth, providing a considerable amount of the Earth's power needs. Private companies would later send up similar stations, which could actually beam down radiation to private moving solar-powered vehicles, recharging them on the run—even at night.

But the private power stations didn't have the technology that later U.S. government stations had—the ability to focus and amplify that solar power into a hideous weapon that could melt cities to the ground in mere minutes. With the arrogance that comes from being the only superpower in the world and from having expanded to include thirty percent of the world's population on six continents, the U.S. military and civilian and industrial powers that oper-

ated the country never even bothered explaining how they
had put this enormous weapon into "weapon-free space."

The Ohio State research indicated that the only way to
control the antiphotosynthesis browning was to obliterate it
instantly so that it could not spread on the wind. On April
15, 2010—there are those who thought income tax reporting day was a fit omen—King City and every living thing
considered to be of value in the ten-mile area around the
city was evacuated, and the space weapon was turned on.

It was as if the sun had been brought to Earth. A blinding
ray—everyone had been given powerful sun-shielding
glasses—took twenty-five minutes to convert the mountain
of trash and King City into a smooth glass knoll ten miles
in diameter.

The immediate crisis was over. But no one could be sure
if the antiphotosynthesis gene was truly destroyed. Perhaps
it had seeped into the underground water system or had
been carried elsewhere by the wind.

With scientists constantly warning about what could happen, governments and laboratories were kept busy anytime
anyone within a thousand miles of the former site of King
City discovered anything that even slightly resembled a
dead or dying plant.

By now the biotechnology giant Amgen had developed
a DNA test for the antiphotosynthesis gene and the assays
were selling like hotcakes. Every laboratory in every state,
city, county, village, and town wanted to have a test available when the next wilted plant came in because the object
was to catch the browning before the "Sun Devil" had to
be employed to sacrifice the countryside.

In fact, three years later, in 2213, a speck of the antiphotosynthesis gene appeared near Coalinga, about twenty-
five miles away. This time only about a thousand acres
were vaporized. In the next fifty years, there would be eighteen discoveries of the gene, one as far away as southern
Utah, and requiring a forty-mile diameter blasting because
it was not picked up early enough.

From space, the western United States looked like a
speckled egg, as sunlight glistened off the black glass that
was dotted over the land.

Most disheartening of all was that science could not figure out a way to turn off the gene chemically or genetically. It was as if the gene knew what human scientists were trying to do and was one step ahead in the evolutionary war for survival—a war with its outcome in doubt that humans in 2266 were still fighting.

23

LET'S GO TAKE OVER ANOTHER WORLD

NABYLA GUERRERO COHANE ADMIRED HERSELF IN THE full-length prismatic mirror which rotated to allow her to see herself from every angle.

"A bit of a sag there," she said to herself, readjusting her bodice. "A couple of wrinkles around the eyes." She squinted and stuck her tongue out at herself. "But otherwise an acceptable package for a hundred-year-old broad."

Of course, Nabyla didn't look one hundred or think one hundred or act one hundred, since a good forty years had been spent in suspended animation, and the wonders of twenty-second century plastic surgery had done a marvelous reshaping job on her hips, breasts, eyes, and neckline. The neck was the giveaway to a person's age. Just counting the creases below the ear—ten years to a crease—was a fairly accurate way to measure, unless the plastic surgeons, especially the gene surgeons, were plying their trade.

Nabyla evaluated herself. *After a couple of drinks, some bar sot might believe I was still in my thirties,* she thought. Realistically, Nabyla knew she could pass for forty, but played her self off as being fiftyish in a crowd that didn't recognize her. And except for those ridiculous twentieth, twenty-fifth, thirtieth and thirty-fifth television anniversary specials of her return to Earth with the Sorgast, no one did recognize her unless they put two and two together when she mentioned she was a retired space explorer.

Redmond was still at her side at most of these functions. He looked distinguished, but no one would question that he was a man in his late sixties, and by the look of the woman on his arm, was robbing the cradle by a good twenty years. The fact that Nabyla was older than Redmond amused her greatly.

Nabyla stepped away from the mirror. *No, you're a pretty good-looking babe for someone who is going to go out and celebrate her one-hundredth birthday,* she thought.

And for my birthday, I've got a great plan, she thought as she left the bedroom and joined the party in her Gaza Coast mansion, overlooking the Mediterranean Sea. Redmond was waiting at the stairs and they descended together, cheered by clinking glasses and robust cheers.

They danced the night away, and as the starlit sky began to lighten and the brilliant points of light faded, Nabyla whispered into the ears of a few guests, asking them to stay for breakfast before they returned to their homes. Nabyla was pleased to see Asorg and Ranan, although their children and grandchildren hadn't made the trip, but she didn't bid them to stay. Somehow, Nabyla thought, they would not like what she was thinking.

A knot of ten people gathered in the spacious kitchen— it would be obscene to refer to it as a breakfast nook, since it was big enough to have sufficed as the entire apartment for a not terribly poor Manhattanite.

She smiled at the gathering. "Can we all keep a secret?" she asked.

"You're pregnant again?" Warrick said, laughing.

All four of Nabyla's and Redmond's children, conceived since their return to Earth, were now out of college, married, and producing grandchildren at scandalous rates, their futures secured by their own intellect and substantial trusts set up by their parents, who were still collecting royalties from their books, animated comic books, merchandising, and other benefits of being interstellar kidnappers.

"No," Nabyla laughed, "I think I've had enough of that chaos." Her voice turned more serious. "I think I'm up for something a little more adventurous. This planet is heading for chaos. We are fast becoming an orb with ten billion people. There are two million people in Gaza City. There are twenty million in New York City, and only the Lord knows how many people live in the São Paulo-Rio de Janeiro metroplex—sixty-eight million in the 2160 census.

"It's getting too crowded. The oceans are rising, the world is heating up—another two degrees in less than half a century. Horrendous epidemics threaten every one of us because some fool gets infected with smallpox." The room nodded as Nabyla stopped and wiped a tear from her eye. One of her grandsons had died in the smallpox epidemic, and a half dozen others were sickened by the disease. She absentmindedly fingered the scar left by the immunization. She saw others do the same.

"What we need is a new place to live, and I don't mean a place on this world." A couple of the guests opened their eyes a bit wider, getting the scent of her direction.

"What we should do is to go to another world that supports life, and begin our own society. It's not too late. It can be done. We can do it."

Several of the couples began to talk to each other, but Nabyla noted with satisfaction that no one started edging toward the door.

"Are you thinking of the Virginis mission?" one asked. After finding humans on Tau Ceti, researchers locked in on Virginis as the next most likely star with an Earth-like planet and a Sol-like sun. But Virginis was thirty-five light-years from Earth. Even with the continuing improvements in interstellar-drive technology, the best anyone could do was forty percent the speed of light, although the experiences of Nabyla's travels and the Tau Ceti expedition indicated that in deep space faster speeds were attainable. Even so, no one was approaching even fifty percent light-speed.

What that meant was that the Virginis mission launched in 2148 wasn't going to get to the star for seventy-five years—2223—and no one would find out what was happening there until 2258. And specimens would not be returned to Earth until 2298 at the earliest. Improvements in the baths and in computerized controls allowed people to stay in the baths for as long as ten years at a stretch (probably indefinitely but no one was going to try it), and then the person would only need a six-month recovery before he or she could be reimmersed. In theory, the trip should age the crew of the Virginis mission only about three years. Of course when they returned to Earth virtually everyone they once knew would be dead.

"No," said Nabyla. "I think we should go where we know the air is good, the planet fruitful, and the natives civilized."

That eliminated Alpha Centauri, where humans had a fifty-fifty chance of being dinner rather than eating dinner.

Nabyla paused. "Tau Ceti Beta."

The guests murmured. The estimates of the population of Tau Ceti Beta were in the neighborhood of one hundred million, spread out across a planet that had twenty percent more land than Earth—before the ice cap melting stole more land to the sea.

Warrick stood up. "So what you are proposing is that we go to Beta and find a nice part of the globe that we can stake out and call our own. That sounds pretty good, but don't you think that most of the good places on that planet have already been occupied? Even the New World on Earth was occupied when Europeans showed up and conquered it. Won't the same thing be true on Beta?"

There was a twinkle in Nabyla's eye that Warrick had seen before, and he knew what the woman was thinking.

Nabyla recounted history: "When Cortez arrived on the shores of Mexico, he was greeted by huge numbers of natives armed with spears and arrows. He had muskets so two hundred men could conquer the land, force its leaders to submit, and then be tortured to death and have the natives of the land hand over all its wealth," she said.

"The difference was technology. Cortez had sixteenth-century technology; the Aztecs had tenth-century technology. When we go to Tau Ceti we will have twenty-second-century technology, they've got second-century technology. We will simply demonstrate why we are fit to move onto the lands that we select as most beneficial to our development,'' she said.

''Uh, what are you going to do to the people who are there now?''

''Don't worry. When they see what some of our weapons can do, and what our technology can do for them, we will be accepted not as conquerors but as deliverers, deities. Besides, we can't eliminate them. We need them to plant, provide food, and run the world we will create. We will direct and the people who we select as our compatriots will joyfully support us. If they don't support us, well, then they can just leave and go somewhere else.

''History has taught us that power corrupts and absolute power corrupts absolutely. We will be the absolute powers on this world, so we must be exceptionally careful not to abuse our 'powers. We will be like gods to these people, and we cannot be cruel gods. While we will rule the planet, we cannot rule alone. We must have subjects who will follow after us, and who will protect us from the others, who will certainly attack us for the good fortune we will bring these people.'' Nabyla was warming up. She'd had this speech ready for months.

Warrick interrupted. ''Nabyla, everything you say is true. Our technology surpasses anything on that planet, especially since the United Nations forbade any trade with any of the planets until a decision can be made on how to treat the indigenous peoples. Of course the U.S. has been debating that since 2090.

''But, Nabyla, all our technology is electronic. It runs on electric power, on electric batteries on direct electricity. There is no electricity on Beta. When our battery power gives out we will be as helpless as the people we rule.''

Nabyla smiled, clapped her hands twice, and a hologram appeared. It was Davis. ''Hi, Nabyla. Warrick, I know you are there. I made this hologram three weeks ago. Most of you know that I'm back in space rounding up asteroids. No, I didn't blow the money, I just like space and I love flying. But I really love Nabyla's plan.

"About now," the hologram continued, "somebody's brought up the problem of operating an electronic system without electricity. Well, let me show you something." Davis vanished and a picture of a space hybrid appeared, towing a satellite. Davis reappeared. "That satellite, ladies and gents, is one of the obsolete power stations that was originally sent up here in 2038. This is a 2045 model that was turned off a couple of years ago. Someone is going to miss it one of these days, but it won't be the government. It'll be one of those kids that are always tracking space junk to try and locate seared metal when it finally comes back to Earth.

"This model is obsolete and turned off, but, my God, it still works. What we are going to do is make our 'temple' on Tau Ceti the place where the power station beams its energy. We'll set it up with enough safety trip devices that anyone who gets within a mile of the 'temple' will be fried to a crisp. As long as we have the 'temple' we will be secure in our power. In addition, I've secured a few of these hybrids so we can always retreat to the ship if things suddenly get hot on the surface.

"We are also going to need a team in space at all times to monitor the signals from do-gooders like the U.N. or do-badders like us who may have the same idea. Nabyla can count on Luba and me. Are the rest of you in or out?" He blinked out of existence.

Nabyla scanned the room. She saw looks of concern on a few faces, but no one seemed rigid. "Davis is ready. Redmond and I are ready. We need to do this fairly soon. You were all selected because you have different and varied experiences in space and on Earth. Everyone is essential, but no one is indispensable. We want you all to come, but we will understand if you don't join us. We know that you won't give us away to the authorities because we have all trusted each other with our lives hundreds of times. We want to leave within three months."

"Awfully soon." "Quick." "No big deal."

Nabyla continued, "Pack some memories, but not many. Give your possessions to your kids because you aren't going to need them up there. Think of what is going to be essential to survive in an area where mass transportation is the number of people you can fit on a beast of burden. Someone is already bringing the Knowledge Disks; and I've stolen my son's sequencer.

"We are off on a voyage of conquest that won't be equaled for centuries. We are going to be the history of a real New World."

She raised her cup of champagne. Her eyes blazed as the others picked up their glasses. "Let us race to the stars. Let us eclipse Columbus. Let us show the Children of the Aliens that their gods have returned.

"To immortality."

And the room responded: "To immortality."

24

CHRONOLOGY

2001
A government-sponsored study is begun to determine why infant mortality rates cannot be lowered in sophisticated societies such as the United States.

2002
The Human Genome Project is completed. Scientists successfully map the entire human gene system, detailing how three billion base pairs of proteins match up to create what is called a human being.

A gene which triggers asthma attacks is discovered.

2003
The gene which codes for the color of a person's eyes is identified.

2004
Resistant bugs—at first thought only to be a danger to hospital patients—are now infecting people in homes, on the street, in airplanes. The death rate climbs to forty percent of those infected.

2005
The space cannon is used to blast powdered foods into space for use by the space-station crews and others.

2006
Rotating wheels on automobiles become standard; parallel parking ceases to be the bane of driver's education courses.

2007
Science and industry team up to find ways of manipulating genes to gain financial rewards.

2008
The reexploration of the Moon begins as a worldwide co-operative project, particularly involving the U.S., Russia, Europe, China, and Japan. Researchers begin regular scientific expeditions to the surface of the Moon.

Wealthy Palm Beach, Florida, rebuilds its beach—for a second time—in attempts to fight the ocean, which relentlessly removes sand from the beach area.

The pharmaceutical industry creates an effective next level of antibiotics that brings the Great VRE Epidemic to a halt.

2009
The world's first surviving octuplets are born and are kept alive in oxygenated fluids for as long as three months until their lungs fully develop.

The first electric car travels from Los Angeles to San Francisco without needing recharging.

2010
A Hollywood superstar with vivid blue-green eyes takes the show-business world by storm and millions of parents clamor to use genetic engineering to give their children the same eye color.

Animals carrying the deadly Ebola fever virus complete the conquest of their range in Africa and the virus can now be found from Nigeria to Tanzania to Angola.

2011
Scientists determine they can manipulate the genes which control skin pigmentation.

Researchers promote the idea of removing the fetus from the womb during the last two months of pregnancy and letting the fetus develop in special incubators.

2012
A vaccine is developed to control asthma; it becomes universal treatment by 2022.

2013
The Clone People begin to establish a secret, clandestine project in Wyoming to create a perfect society with perfect children.

2014
Electric cars are being sold that have cruising ranges of a thousand miles, making them cost-effective as well as environmentally friendly.

2015
Extensive genetic tests are able to determine who is likely to develop diseases as common as breast cancer to relatively uncommon illnesses such as neuroblastoma.

2016
A group of scientists and science-fiction activists create the GiSAS movement, a religion that claims that mankind descended from a roving band of interstellar humanoids who impregnate creatures on a planet and then abandon the new creatures to fend for themselves. Members of the movement are ridiculed and harassed.

2017
Zebra mussels, the scourge of North American waterways, are blamed for fouling water inlet and outlet pipes all the way down the Allegheny to the Ohio to the Mississippi River to New Orleans. Government agencies spend hun-

dreds of millions of dollars in attempts to find biological ways of stopping the spread of the mussel.

Polio is eradicated around the world.

2018
Scientists find the genes that control attention deficit disorder.

New York City bans fuel-burning motor vehicles south of Ninety-sixth Street. Parking meters include plugs for recharging while a person shops.

DNA is extracted from the semifossilized bone marrow of Neandertal bodies discovered in Austrian caves.

2019
The lung cancer gene is isolated, ironically giving renewed life to cigarette manufacturers because people can now tell who will get cancer from cigarettes.

The zebra mussel is in the Colorado River, panicking Southern California. If the zebra mussel clogs the Colorado River water inlet pipes, Los Angeles will die of thirst—quickly.

2020
A Tennessee lawyer uncovers evidence that insurance companies are violating the law by denying medical coverage to those who have genetic abnormalities.

2021
Two of Jupiter's moons collide and explode, resulting in deadly asteroid showers that threaten to destroy Earth.

2022
A biological weapon—a zebra mussel specific worm—to fight the zebra mussel is developed, but before it can be used researchers find that the mussel is an avid devourer of algae and has done such a good job in cleaning up major lakes and rivers that the antimussel weapon is shelved.

A third attempt—the mother of all beaches, extending the beach four hundred feet from shore for one mile, is constructed at Palm Beach at a cost of a billion dollars.

2023
The clone project establishes its first schools and government operations and is totally ignored by the rest of the world.

A march of more than three hundred thousand people turns ugly in Hartford, Connecticut, and the mob burns down a major insurance company in the Gene Riots of 2023.

2024
The Hadj Epidemic. A devout Islamic peasant from a jungle village in Nigeria boards a jumbo jet in Lagos to make the pilgrimage to Mecca. The man becomes violently ill on the plane, and although the Ebola virus can only be spread by contact allowing the virus to penetrate the skin, he manages to infect a dozen people on the plane before it lands in Mecca. Instead of being hospitalized he is carried by other Muslims to the sacred monuments of the faith, where scores of others are infected. In a worst-case scenario, more than one hundred people are infected with Ebola by the man who eventually dies in a Saudi Arabia hospital. The people with the disease are scattered throughout the world. Eventually close to one thousand Ebola deaths will be attributed to this one case and world governments will spend a quarter of a billion dollars in a frantic attempt to track down the virus carriers before the infections can be spread.

The town of Palm Beach closes the entrances to its ocean beaches and spends several hundred million dollars reinforcing the seawall. Instead of a beach, Palm Beach constructs a twenty-foot-wide, half-mile-long concrete barrier to hold back the sea.

2025
Insurance companies are prohibited from writing any form of health insurance, as the government assumes all health-care coverage.

2030
Virtually all fetuses are removed from the womb and are placed in special placental incubators, where they are given carefully controlled nutrition so they reach term well nour-

ished, avoiding delivery table illness and trauma and giving mothers a chance to overcome postpartum depression.

2032
Scientists learn how to manipulate genes to prevent attention deficit disorder from occurring in children.

Scores of the anti–zebra mussel worm are destroyed. Connecticut names the zebra mussel as the State Mollusk; other states follow.

2037
The Microsoft Cartel expands again, this time into toy manufacturing by acquiring Mattel. One of the first devices the new brain trust comes up with is an inexpensive DNA sequencing device that gives grade-school and middle-school students the ability to develop exciting experiments in genetic engineering and identification. The sequencer revolutionizes children's interest in science and results in several new discoveries which help change medical and plant science.

2038
The first space-based solar power stations go on-line, designed to take solar energy in space and redirect it to solar collectors on Earth, providing a considerable amount of the Earth's power needs.

2040
Genetic manipulation eradicates breast cancer and ovarian cancer through control of the p53 gene mechanisms.

The last case of smallpox occurred sixty years earlier and world medical staffs believe it has been eradicated; hospitals worldwide discard their stores of smallpox vaccine.

2043
The sexually transmitted disease chlamydia, one of the world's greatest causes of female infertility, is eradicated as United States drug manufacturers provide an effective one-dose cure for the disease—available at high cost since 1990—free to undeveloped areas of the world. There is no

connection, United Nations officials say, between the free
distribution of the antibiotic and the U.N.'s decision to dis-
band a twenty-five-year-old task force scrutinizing how
drugs are manufactured and distributed around the world.

2044

The last of the women present at the fateful party which
led to the death of Mary Jo Kopechne in Senator Edward
M. Kennedy's car dies. None of the women ever disclose
any details of the event which scuttled Kennedy's chance
to be president of the U.S.

2048

The first Moon-based telescopes aimed at locating wayward
asteroids are manned by the forerunners of major colonies
on the Moon. The first colony consists of about twenty-five
families, all connected in some manner to the operation of
the telescopes.

2051

A second Moon colony, dedicated to mining operations on
the Moon and the receipt of mineral-rich asteroids, is established. It will soon outgrow the first settlement.

2053

Operation of Moon-based telescopes goes out for bids to
industries, which develop a system to locate the largest of
the asteroids, map them, round them up with asteroid cowboys, and herd the rocks back to the Moon, where they can
be mined.

2060

The Cloninger experiment collapses.

The first metal-fabricating plant goes on-line on the
Moon's surface, powered by solar energy. The production
of airtight containers allows comfortable living quarters in
space.

2065
General Motors and NASA develop the direct solar car battery-recharge system. Space satellites direct sunlight directly to vehicle solar cells mounted on the roofs of cars, recharging the cars on the run.

2068
It's revealed that the actress responsible for a generation of blue-green-eyed children wore colored contact lenses to give her eyes that distinctive color.

The IBM-Exxon space exploration team heads to Alpha Centauri to determine if life-forms exist on a planet circling the star. It will take eighteen years for the mission to reach the planet.

2070
The colonization of Mars begins.

2075
The Moon colonies employ tens of thousands of people, and minor colonies are established on Mars and the stable moons of Jupiter.

2077
The Aldabra Islands in the Pacific Ocean vanish following a cyclone, victims of rising ocean levels, warmer temperatures, and more destructive tropical storms.

2082
The Sheraton Luna opens on the Moon as hundreds of tourists invade the Moon.

2083
A hurricane churns off Palm Beach for three days, soaking the area with thirty-six inches of rain and hurling tides and waves up to fifteen feet high against the town's billion-dollar seawall. The barricade loses.

2090
The first reports of humanoid existence on another planet reach Earth, and begin a period in which dozens of free-

booters travel the void between stars in multiyear journeys in order to reap the profits and fame of being able to bring back a live specimen of another race.

2094
The discovery of humanoids on Alpha Centauri gives the GiSAS sect momentum. The cult's motto: Do unto others as you would have them do unto you—because the powerful beings that created mankind, beings that were at least three hundred thousand years more advanced than we, are going to return and punish those who are evil.

2097
The hottest toy of the century in Microsoft-Mattel's marriage of the educational DNA sequencer to Scientist Barbie.

2099
The incredible public-relations success of the IBM-Exxon mission to Alpha Centauri leads the Microsoft Cartel to begin the $34 billion Tau Ceti expedition. Tau Ceti, about eleven light-years from Earth, has a Sol-like sun, and space-based telescopes have identified at least two planets circling Tau Ceti. The mission is expected to take just over twenty years to reach Tau Ceti.

2095
Virtually every vehicle on the road is run by solar electric energy.

2099
On the last day of the twenty-first century, the city council of Galveston closes down the city, deeding all city-owned property, including virtually all homes and businesses that had been abandoned during the past twenty years, victims of a slow but insistent increase in the level of the oceans, to the state of Texas.

2100
The United Nations, with the concurrence of virtually every independent state as well as agreements from colonists on

the Moon, Mars, and the moons of Jupiter, agree to harsh penalties for anyone who harms intelligent humanoids from other planets. The laws have absolutely no effect in stopping unauthorized travels to these planets in hopes of capturing humanoids.

Scientists find that global warming trends confirmed at the end of the twentieth century have continued and the planet is about two degrees warmer than one hundred years earlier. The news excites virtually no one.

2102
The combination of rising oceanic water levels and a 150-mile-an-hour cyclone pushing a storm surge twenty-five feet high kills six million people in Bangladesh. The government abandons more than a quarter of the nation's land—most of it now regularly inundated. The pressure of 168 million people living in such tight, unsanitary quarters results in a cascade of plagues that kills millions.

2108
The first humanoids to be taken alive from the Centauri system are kidnapped by freebooters, although no one on Earth finds out about the capture for eighteen years.

Palm Beach condemns homes along the seawall which is breached by virtually every dinky rainstorm that crops up.

2116
Following four years of warm winters in which the temperatures fail to fall below forty degrees Fahrenheit, St. Louis and parts of the Midwest are hit by an outbreak of dengue hemorraghic fever, an outgrowth of global warming which has extended the range of mosquitoes carrying the virus.

2117
The wave of pandemics in Bangladesh subsides, but the population of the country, once 168 million, has been reduced to less than a hundred million.

2127

The humanoids captured on Alpha Centauri's planet are brought to Earth while the crew that kidnapped the humanoids are, after considerable negotiations in which a great deal of money is bargained against serious time in confinement, substantially rewarded.

2128

DNA analysis of the blood from the aliens shows that they are true Homo sapiens, possibly being closer to modern day man in genetic structure than even Neandertal man.

GiSAS conventions grow exponentially following the DNA reports.

The Sorgast settle in Sedona, Arizona, after the birth of their daughter Ranas.

2130

The first receipt of transmissions from Tau Ceti find that humanoid life exists on two planets in that system in societies that are further advanced than on Alpha Centauri but are still well behind Earth in technological achievement. Several Cetians are persuaded to return to Earth.

The Tau Ceti mission takes along DNA-sequencing equipment and sends a digitized DNA code sample across space. The sequencing again proves that the humanoids on Tau Ceti are human.

2131

Asorg Sorgast publishes his book on how people can talk to their elders. It sells well, but few can achieve communication with the ''dead.''

2132

With the information from Tau Ceti, the scientific community determines that, indeed, all four groups of humanoids—Tau Ceti-a, Tau Ceti-b, Alpha Centauri, and Earth must have been populated by the same species. Somehow an unknown people had impregnated creatures on these planets and then had gone away, allowing these colonies to develop as the various ecologies on the planets allowed.

2133

Remarkably, the proof that they were correct in their assumptions, reduced the growth rate of the GiSAS, but not the ferocity of their members' attempts to convert the rest of the world to their cult.

2138

A church near Fort Smith, Arkansas, is burned as the religious war breaks out.

2139

More than five hundred churches of all denominations, including an occasional synagogue or mosque, suffer damaging attacks, and scores are destroyed.

2140

A GiSAS mob in Evergreen, Colorado, attacks an evangelical church service, leaving more than 100 men, women, and children dead.

2145

The Tau Ceti mission returns to the solar system, but the decision to land on Earth is delayed more than twenty years owing to the religious holocaust. The Tau Ceti visitors reside on the Moon until the Earth becomes less of an embarrassment for them to visit.

2147

Sorgan Sorgast is married to the daughter of a major motion picture star in a cast of thousands ceremony that is broadcast live on all eleven all-news channels. The wedding is protested by sheet-covered groups who declare that it's against God's law for green-skinned aliens to have intercourse with Caucasian women. The protesters are pelted with wedding cake by departing wedding guests. A picture taken of a mongrel dog licking icing off the hood of a slumped-over protester wins the year's Pulitzer prize for photography.

2148
After finding humans on Tau Ceti, scientists began the 140-to-150-year round-trip mission to Virginis, the next most likely star with an Earth-like planet and a Sol-like sun—thirty-five light-years from Earth.

2151
Ranas Sorgast is married in a quiet ceremony in Tahiti to the son of a Tibetan crystal salesman.

A Russian relic hunter uncovers a frozen coffin and unleashes smallpox into an unvaccinated, unprotected world.

2152
In Moscow alone, eight million—almost half of the city's seventeen million residents—die from the virulent strain of smallpox that gallops across the metropolis.

2158
A Papal decree finds no inconsistencies between the Church's teachings and the existence of humans on other planets. The decree eases the ferocity of the religious war by calling for peace on all sides.

2060
Health officials finally claim that the smallpox epidemic is under control, but estimate that six hundred million have died from the disease. While the outbreak is controlled, smallpox is not eradicated.

The world census puts the population of the globe at 9.1 billion—even after the smallpox terror—and determines that the largest metropolis is the São Paulo-Rio de Janeiro metroplex, with sixty-eight million people.

2164
The Tau Cetis, originally numbering eighteen people, now having grown to thirty, are finally allowed to visit Earth, and are accepted as citizens there. They opt to be kept in a separate community, and seek inclusion into the aloof Hutterite sects of Washington state, which have weathered the religious wars well simply by ignoring their existence.

2166

After a bloodbath that claims 212 million lives around the world, the twenty-five-year-long GiSAS Wars are considered over.

On her one hundredth birthday, Nabyla Cohane and a crew of ten and their families—a total of forty people—embark on a secret mission: the armed overthrow of Tau Ceti Beta.

2167

An epidemiologist successfully tracks the smallpox epidemic to its source, the coffin of a woman who died of the disease in 1850. The strain of the virus she contracted was able to survive in her body and possessions for the three hundred years it took before she was discovered, and that strain would be responsible for the deaths of six hundred million people in a ten-year period.

2171

A third-grade student in Amarillo, Texas, playing with his father's newest Microsoft-Mattel toy, the StarFinder, has trouble finding an obsolete space satellite. Even though he knows the listed coordinates for the satellite and has entered the data into the StarFinder, he still comes up with a blank. He calls Microsoft customer support and sets off a month-long investigation which concludes that the satellite must have been stolen.

2176

Research teams find that the two Tau Ceti families, mixed Centauri-Earth children, and the spouse of Sorgan Sorgast are able to engage in regular discussions with elders.

2179

Scientists say they have isolated a gene which they believe triggers the production of an enzyme that throws a genetic switch allowing the brain to pierce the boundary between the tactile world and the other dimension.

The GiSAS convention offers a billion-dollar reward to the scientist who can develop a way to trigger the cascade of events that opens the door to the elders. The reward is matched by Bristol-Myers Squibb Merck Bayer, the interplanetary pharmaceutical giant.

2188
A relatively small earthquake, measuring 6.8 on the Richter scale, demolishes homes, schools, and a hospital around King City, California. The residents rebuild, using the earthquake debris as the foundation for a new landfill site outside the city limits.

2196
The compound to open the door to the elders is synthesized, but it takes another ten years before its toxicity and correct dosage is determined.

2204
A message picked up by Earth SETI-monitoring equipment indicates that mercenaries from Earth have invaded, conquered, and subjected the people of Tau Ceti Beta. Earth governments debate what the proper response should be to the obvious violation of international convention.

2206
The compound opening the door to the elders is marketed, but contact cannot be made with long-lost relatives. Asorg Sorgast explains that contact has to be made immediately after death to prevent the elders from drifting away.

The King City landfill is closed, but attempts to sod it and turn the landfill into a playground are stymied by the browning of new growths.

2209
The King City landfill is a wasteland, and experts are called in to find out what is causing the browning of the landfill and adjacent areas.

2210

King City is evacuated and the Sun Devil, a secret military weapon, turns the city, its landfill, and an area ten miles in diameter into a smooth glass knoll.

2213

The browning gene is isolated near Coalinga, about twenty-five miles away from King City; about one thousand acres are vaporized.

2223

The Virginis mission arrives at the solar system, and again finds a humanoid life form living in a hostile environment. The humanoids have developed a technology more advanced than Alpha Centauri, but have failed to come close to achieving the civilization of the Tau Cetis. Paradoxically, the planet abounds in natural resources. So rich is the planet in precious metals that the captain has to put down a near mutiny among crew members who want to stay and plunder the planet. No humanoids can be coaxed aboard the ship. Crew members are coy about what they have discovered in messages sent back home, messages that won't arrive for thirty-five years.

2240

After 218 votes over thirty-five years of discussion in which no action can be agreed upon, the United Nations decides to send a mission to Tau Ceti Beta to investigate charges of outside intervention by Earthling mercenaries. It takes an additional ten years to raise funds for the expedition and another three to hammer out the goals and aims.

2253

The U.N. mission, once a liberation party, then a rescue party, and now a fact-finding group, blasts off for Tau Ceti Beta, on a trip that will not end until after the next century begins.

2266
The browning gene has been found in eighteen more places since 2213, one as far away as southern Utah, which requires a forty-mile-diameter blasting because it is not noticed in a timely fashion.

FASCINATING BOOKS
OF SPIRITUALITY
AND PSYCHIC DIVINATION

CLOUD NINE: A DREAMER'S DICTIONARY
by Sandra A. Thomson
77384-8/$6.99 US/$7.99 Can

SECRETS OF SHAMANISM:
TAPPING THE SPIRIT POWER
WITHIN YOU
by Jose Stevens, Ph.D. and Lena S. Stevens
75607-2/$5.99 US/$6.99 Can

THE LOVERS' TAROT
*by Robert Mueller, Ph.D., and Signe E. Echols, M.S.,
with Sandra A. Thomson*
76886-0/$11.00 US/$13.00 Can

SEXUAL ASTROLOGY
by Marlene Masini Rathgeb
76888-7/$11.00 US/$15.00 Can

SPIRITUAL TAROT: SEVENTY-EIGHT
PATHS TO PERSONAL DEVELOPMENT
*by Signe E. Echols, M.S., Robert Mueller, Ph.D.,
and Sandra A. Thomson*
78206-5/$12.00 US/$16.00 Can

Zecharia Sitchin's
The Earth Chronicles

BOOK I: THE 12TH PLANET
39362-X/$6.99 US/$8.99 CAN

This revolutionary work brings together lost, antediluvian texts, ancient cosmologies, and newly discovered celestial maps to reach the shocking conclusion that we are descendants of a superior race from the 12th planet.

BOOK II: THE STAIRWAY TO HEAVEN
63339-6/$6.99 US/$8.99 CAN

BOOK III: THE WARS OF GODS AND MEN
89585-4/$6.99 US/$8.99 CAN

BOOK IV: THE LOST REALMS
75890-3/$6.99 US/$8.99 CAN

BOOK V: WHEN TIME BEGAN
77071-7/$6.99 US/$8.99 CAN

And Don't Miss the Companion Volumes:

GENESIS REVISITED: IS MODERN SCIENCE CATCHING UP WITH ANCIENT KNOWLEDGE?
76159-9/$6.99 US/$8.99 CAN

DIVINE ENCOUNTERS: A GUIDE TO VISIONS, ANGELS, AND OTHER EMISSARIES
78076-3/$6.50 US/$8.50 CAN